MW00941342

Strategic spiritual warfare

TURNING POINT
BREAKTHROUGH PRAYERS

Anointed warfare prayers for your spiritual
transformation in 90 days

Joseph A. Dodjro

O light of favor of God

shine forth into Pearl's
life this season, in
Jesus' name!

Aluleph

Pastor Joseph

Edmonton, AB APR 22, 2012

TABLE OF CONTENTS
Part One

Part Two

Part One

Preface

Breaking the cycle of bondage in 90 days
through spiritual warfare

Friend, you are about to embark on a journey that will change your life as you know it positively, spectacularly, and so dramatically that your friends will be asking you, "What happened to you?" I want to share with you a way of praying that will enable you to achieve significant breakthrough in your life, right from your own prayer closet.

After the disciples of Jesus watched Him for a few years, preaching all day and praying all night, they pulled him aside and told Him, "Teach us how to pray." What they were saying in essence is, "We, too, want to get results, and teach the secrets of prayer. What do you say when you pray?"

Also, in Matthew 17:14-21, a man brought his demon-possessed son to Jesus' disciples. They could not help the boy. It did not mean the disciples did not pray. They prayed, but nothing happened and so the man took his son to Jesus. Jesus rebuked and cast out the powerful demon behind the boy's epilepsy, and the demon was gone. The boy was healed and well again. This great miracle caused the disciples of Jesus to go to Jesus again and ask Him the question, "What is going on here? You taught us how to pray, and we prayed, but the boy was not healed when we prayed." Just as it was with the disciples of Jesus, so it is with you. Are you praying about your situation, but too many times nothing is happening? It is for this reason that we bring you these prayers that go directly to your situation. When you pray these prayers on your own or with a group, you will experience change in ways you have not before. These turning point breakthrough prayers will speak to the core problems associated with your situations.

Dedication

T his prayer manual is the work of the Holy Spirit – our helper, counselor, strengthener, advocate, intercessor, and friend. Thank you, Holy Spirit, for being the inspiration behind these life-transforming prayers.

INSTRUCTION ON HOW TO PRAY THESE PRAYERS

1) Get ready as if you were a real soldier preparing for battle, for you truly are a soldier in God's victorious army. Stand up and remain standing throughout the duration of your prayer session.

2) Start your session with songs of praise and worship of your choice. Make your choice deliberately by including songs that mention and exalt the name of Jesus. Choose songs about the blood of Jesus, and the power in the blood. If you don't know any songs that fit into this category, play a CD that has these songs. Play them until you can sing them on your own. During these prayers, it is recommended that you sing the songs yourself with your own voice, for deliverance is about coming out of captivity, and coming out of captivity means that you want the enemy of our soul to hear your voice as being more than a conqueror.

3) Pray an introductory prayer which should include thanking God, inviting the presence of the Holy Spirit during your session, sprinkling the blood of Jesus over and around your immediate envi-

ronment (Hebrews 12:23-25), and releasing God's angels to protect you and minister to you during this prayer session and throughout your program. Thank the Lord for the victory He has already given you over the powers of darkness. End your introductory prayer by saying, "In the name of Jesus, I have prayed."

4) Now acquaint yourself with this entire book, especially the operational instructions therein. Then select your section based on your spiritual need or the title of the section.

5) Now that you have made your selection, read suggested scripture passages aloud. As you read, open your spirit to receive the message the Holy Spirit is bringing and will bring to your attention during this session. As you read, look for verses that stand out, as if they are jumping out to you during your reading. Highlight these verses and make them the focus for your further spiritual meditation. Add your own list of scriptural passages to our suggested list. Referring to and keeping a list of scriptures with your prayers is vital. The scriptures are the life of your prayers. Continue to read the scriptures before and during your prayers.

6) Ready? Set? Go! Take one prayer point at a time. Read aloud the prayer point three times, always ending with "in the name of Jesus," as it is throughout this prayer manual. After repeating the same line three times, you should have memorized that prayer line. If you have not, then repeat it again, until you can repeat it with your eyes closed. Now, with eyes closed, repeat the same selected prayer point for a minimum of five minutes nonstop, for starters. For sea-

soned prayer warriors, you may pray a single prayer point longer; certainly do so, the longer the better.

7) We have received reports and testimonies of spectacular spiritual breakthroughs from believers who have prayed one single prayer point, some for one hour, some for three hours. Believers in need of deliverance who have prayed repeatedly in the past, and sought deliverance in the past, have reported spectacular miracles when they prayed the same prayer point. Some prayed for an hour, others prayed for three hours. It is up to you how long you stay with each prayer point.

8) When you pray these prayers, we recommend that you pray them at night for ten nights in a row. Prayer works any time of the day, but with these warfare prayers, our experience has been that believers report tremendous spiritual breakthrough, including significant clarification in their dreams, and divine revelations by night, especially when they go to bed immediately after these prayers.

9) Of course, we encourage you to use these prayers as a guide and a kick-start for your day-to-day warfare prayer strategies. If after praying them you receive revelations through dreams at night, study these dreams and formulate your own prayer point to suit the dream or the revelation you have received. To this end, it is also recommended that you keep a dream journal to facilitate a strategic follow-up to your dreams through targeted prayers, revelations received after your prayer, and subsequent necessary prayer actions that need to be taken.

For example, if after praying these prayers aggressively for a few nights you see images in your dream that deal with finances, it means that there are spiritual thieves, devourers, takers, stealers and robbers assigned to your finances and resources. You should then switch your prayer point by standing boldly for three nights in a row against devourers attached to your finances and handiwork. Or perhaps, after praying these prayers, you have a dream that has something to do with your relationship or ministry. Immediately set aside three nights in a row to deal with that particular revelation about that area of your life before continuing on to the selected section you are working on. Always map out your strategy before you begin.

Perhaps you want to take a whole day or night to pray one session. Or you may want to tackle an entire title in this book in one session, praying each prayer point for five minutes at a time.

Whatever your strategy is, go for it, but always keep your focus strong. Stick with each prayer point enough to know that you have achieved something before moving on to the next prayer point.

10) Watch out! When you decide to set ten nights for your deliverance, the first night you will feel like a mighty man of valor. You will even go beyond your own appointed time and still feel like going on and on. And because you have created a lot of havoc in the camp of the enemy, you will feel empowered to continue on aggressively like that on subsequent nights. The second night! Ah, the second night! The enemy will throw everything at you, including the kitchen sink, sending his retaliatory forces against you.

You are forewarned. Do not be discouraged by these attacks. You may become strangely tired the second night and not feel like continuing. Everything that can go wrong on your schedule may start to go wrong on this second night. Know that you are in a battle. It is because you have launched a battle against the enemy's battle. Remember that he is not going to let you have your victory without a fight. Do not give in because of these retaliatory tactics of Satan. Go on. Fight. Fight for your destiny.

11) Let not your heart be troubled. Once you've conquered these roadblocks of the second and even the third night, unyielding and resolute, you will discover that the remaining seven nights will just come to you naturally. It is your time. Do not let the enemy of your soul delay your breakthrough even one more day.

12) Always end your prayer session with a song of thanksgiving. Let the enemy know that you believe in your deliverance, that you believe in your victory, and that you believe in it so much that you are celebrating in advance before the spiritual and the physical come together.

13) These prayers will work for you. Just go straight into your prayer closet and you will find out you can receive miracles right there in your house, for the words of power are now spoken from your mouth.

14) Let me emphasize again the need for you to be strategic and specific in your prayer time. Jesus didn't rebuke every storm (that would be bad news for the weatherman and the weather channel),

nor did he curse every fig tree (we wouldn't have any fig trees). He rebuked only a specific storm and cursed only a specific fig tree. Attack a specific prayer need at a time until victory comes.

Note: If, during the reading of these prayers, you come across terminology that is outside of your understanding, either through cultural differences or differences in theological training, experience, and worship practices, please contact our ministry for explanation.

Joseph A. DODJRO
Exhorter, Prophetic Intercessor, Deliverance minister

CLEANSING AND STRENGTHENING YOUR INNER MAN

Scripture Reading: Psalm 32; Romans 12:2

Romans 12:2 And do not be conformed to this world, but be transformed by the renewing of your mind, that you may prove what is that good and acceptable and perfect will of God.

As close as King David was with God, he always prayed, asking God to cleanse him. We too should adopt the same attitude, righteousness and purity, by asking God to cleanse us from all sins of commission and omission before we engage with the enemy in battle.

Also use Psalm 32 as a guide, reading it aloud before starting this session.

1. Worship your way to His Presence for 15 minutes or more.

2. O Lord my God, in the name of Jesus, remove whatever the enemy has planted in my life to make me sin against you.

3. Holy Spirit, expose everything the enemy has planted in my life to make me walk against the will of God for my life, in the name of Jesus.

4. Every foundational stronghold on my holiness and purity is destroyed in the name of Jesus.

5. Holy Ghost fire, remove the seed of sin and iniquity out of my life, in the name of Jesus.

6. Holy Spirit, send your fire to my root to consume all lines of darkness and sin, in the name of Jesus.

7. O Lord my God, give me power to subdue sin at all time in the name of Jesus.

8. Any power attracting sin into my life, be arrested, in the name of Jesus.

9. O Heavenly Father, surround me with your love and let every arrow of sin and iniquity against me be sent back to the senders, in the name of Jesus.

10. Every agent of iniquity operating in my home and life, be arrested and be judged, in the name of Jesus.

11. Every habitual sin that wants to swallow my destiny is wiped off by the blood of Jesus, in the name of Jesus.

12. I remove all garments of habitual sin from my life, in the name of Jesus.

13. O Lord my God, clothe me with a robe of holiness and purity, in the name of Jesus.

14. Every Holy Ghost fire quencher assigned to monitor me, perish in the name of Jesus.

15. O Lord my God, arise and let all household strongmen opposing the fulfillment of my destiny be scattered into desolation, in the name of Jesus.

16. All demonic alliances operating against me, scatter in the name of Jesus.

17. All African, Asian, North American, European, and other international associations of demons fighting and opposing my destiny and calling, I command you to fight against each other, in the name of Jesus.

18. O Lord my God, let the grip and power of Jezebel in this city be powerless over my life, in the name of Jesus.

19. Every evil power programmed against my life and calling, be deprogrammed, in the name of Jesus.

20. You rod of stagnation and non-accomplishment assigned to oppose me, perish in the name of Jesus.

21. All lines of darkness in this city opposing my life and calling are consumed by fire from the presence of the Sovereign Lord, who created heaven and earth, in the name of Jesus.

22. Satanic prophecy presently active and operating in my life, perish to the root, in the name of Jesus.

23. O Lord my God, assign to me legions of angels to minister to me wherever I go in the name of Jesus.

24. All ways of the ungodly into my life, perish in the name of Jesus.

25. All wicked satanic agents preventing me from moving forward, in the authority of the name of Jesus, are dashed into pieces.

26. I silence the raging of the wicked against me, in the name of the Lord Jesus.

27. Every power, spirit or personality projecting heaviness and weariness over my soul, be shattered by fire in the name of the Lord Jesus.

28. Every power casting stumbling blocks in front of me is smitten by the Arm of the Lord, in the name of the Lord Jesus.

29. O my soul, I command you to come out of captivity, in the authority of the name of Jesus.

30. O Lord my God, do something new and marvelous in my life today, in the name of Jesus.

WARFARE PRAYERS FOR PASTORS, EVANGELISTS, AND OTHER CHURCH LEADERS BEFORE A SCHEDULED CHURCH EVENT (CRUSADE, CONVENTION, REVIVAL MEETING, ETC.).

A church event, be it a prayer meeting, a Sunday regular service, a choir practice, an evangelistic meeting, church planting crusade, a convention or convocation, whatever the gathering may be, as long as it is a gathering of Bible-believing, born again, praying Christians, it does not go unnoticed in the demonic world. From the moment a praying church plans a program to the time and day of the delivery of that program, Satan and his acolytes start to plan all sorts of distractions, attacks, confusion, and sabotage to frustrate the plans of God's people, and to prevent the saints from glorifying God.

As a matter of personal observation, having been in the church environment of four continents, I noticed that nine out every ten churches put more time into planning church programs than they put into praying for these events before and during them. It should not be so.

I have been to too many churches on Sunday or on a big day, when all of sudden key musical equipment stops. If it is not the equipment's malfunction, it is the lighting, or the sound, or it is problems with people, like something between group members, i.e., choir members. These crises do not just happen naturally; they are almost always satanic attacks. As it is often said in the scriptures, the kingdom of our God suffers violence on a daily basis, and only the violent Christian in spirit can overthrow this violence against the people of God. I bring you these prayers for you to use before, during, and even after any church programs. Use them to stand against the plans of the enemy in your midst.

For maximum effect, these prayer points are to be used by the entire prayer group in charge of the meeting. For example, before Sunday service, the worship team and/or the prayer team should pray these prayers. Or before a women's conference or men's or youth gathering, a select group of people, a prayer team should gather and prayer these prayers for several days before the event.

In lieu of a prayer group, the pastor or minister in charge should pray these prayers fervently for several nights before any planned event. Pray these prayers. I know you will contact us with your testimonies regarding these prayers. It is your time. Enjoy the goodness of the Lord in the land of His inheritance for you. Pray.

Scripture Reading: Matthew 11:12; Hosea 12:13
Matthew 11:12 - And from the days of John the Baptist until now the kingdom of heaven suffers violence, and the violent take it by force.

1. O Lord our God, let all plans of the kingdom of darkness for this upcoming meeting (crusade, church service, revival meeting, convention, etc.) be dismantled in the name of Jesus.
2. O God, arise and bring this gathering to a total success in the name of Jesus.
3. Anywhere workers of iniquity are praying against us, let their own prayers work against them, in the name of Jesus.
4. Every strongman of darkness against the gospel of Jesus in this city is arrested, in the name of Jesus.
5. Let the blood of Jesus be released upon every street in this city for the sake of this gathering, in the name of Jesus.
6. For the sake of this gathering, let the blood of Jesus be sprinkled upon every household in this city that is appointed to attend this event.
7. Holy Spirit, scatter every stronghold of darkness standing against this gathering, in the name of Jesus.
8. Every satanic agent assigned to attack this meeting is blinded, in the name of Jesus.

9. Every satanic gate blocking people coming to the meeting, be pulled down in the name of Jesus.

10. Holy Spirit, advertise this meeting to all the right hearts in this city, in the name of Jesus.

11. Holy Spirit, make all needs and expenditures known to the right people related to this meeting, in the name of Jesus

12. Any worldly programs or entertainment spirits that desire to come up during our programs, we prophesy against you; you shall not be established, in Jesus' name.

13. Angels of the Living God, gather all the right souls for this meeting, in the name of Jesus.

14. Holy Spirit, from the beginning to the end of the programs, take control in the name of Jesus.

15. Anointing of healing and deliverance come upon the congregation on that day, in the name of Jesus.

16. O Lord our God, let the heaven of this city be open for the benefit of your kingdom, in the name of Jesus.

17. Spirit of error and mistake, each time we are gathered, we bind you from the beginning to the end of our programs, in the name of Jesus.

18. In the blood of Jesus, we soak the choir, orchestra, band, all musicians and their equipment, all ushers, and the altar.

19. Any power bent to create confusion, mistrust, or uneasiness among choir members, we bind you with fetters of God, in the name of Jesus.

20. It is illegal for powers of darkness to show up where children of the Living God are gathered. Therefore, I destroy all demons and association of demons in our midst right now, in the mighty name of our Lord Jesus.

21. Every satanic gathering against this gathering, be scattered in Jesus' name.

22. O Lord our God, give our choir members special anointing and an excellent spirit for everyone in fellowship, in the name of Jesus.

23. O Lord our God, let your Holy Spirit be our protocol officer during all our gatherings, in the name of Jesus.

24. Holy Spirit, arise and create a divine unity, coordination and harmony among ushers and workers during all our gatherings, in the name of Jesus.

25. O Lord our God, give our technical officers divine wisdom and discernment during all our gatherings.

26. O Lord, provide for all our financial needs for the organization of this meeting, in the name of Jesus.

27. O Lord our God, your word says you have many people in this city. We know that many of these people are not with us who are supposed to be here because the enemy is opposing them.

28. Holy Spirit, arise and release these souls into this ministry for the Lord our God has appointed them for His work, in the name of Jesus.

29. We resist and reject pollution in this ministry, in the name of Jesus.

30. O Lord our God, let all those who are testifying against your glory in this ministry know that you are God.

31. Satan will not remove me where the Lord has placed me in ministry, in the name of Jesus.

End your prayer section by asking the Holy Spirit to protect your portion in ministry in the name of Jesus.

WHAT YOU CAN EXPECT as you pray this session

As you pray these prayer points regularly before each of your programs, you will notice a difference in unusual distractions that often occur during your services. You will also notice an increase in the anointing of His presence amongst you. And more notable will be the total disappearance of frustration among team members towards each other. And where there is lack of frustration, there is joy, joy unspeakable, full of glory. That is your portion in the name of Jesus.

DEFEATING THE SPIRIT OF PHARAOH

Scripture Reading: Exodus 6:10-11; Exodus 7:1-4; Exodus 8:28; Exodus 10:8; Psalm 71:7.

Exodus 6:10-11- And the LORD spoke to Moses, saying, 11 "Go in, tell Pharaoh king of Egypt to let the children of Israel go out of his land."

C aptive spirits enjoy keeping their victims under their regime for as long as they can with no desire of ever letting them go. And if the captives ever make an attempt for freedom or escape, they are severely reprimanded by their captors. A typical case of collective captivity in the Bible is that of the children of Israel and their 430 years of captivity, bondage, and servitude in Egypt. Just as it was in the case of the House of Israel in Egypt, the spirit of Pharaoh is still alive and well today. The spirit of Pharaoh is responsible for keeping saints in captivity for years, even decades; keeping them under captivity with no intention of letting them go.

People under the influence of the spirit of Pharaoh have no way of setting themselves free. To completely defeat the spirit of Pharaoh in your life, or in any department of your life, we recommend that you 1) contact us about hosting deliverance workshops in your city. In the workshops these prayers are prayed in groups along with other prayer warriors; 2) form a believers' prayer group with the sole purpose of praying these prayers in one accord.

1. Every active spirit of Pharaoh operating in my life, destroy yourself in the name of Jesus.

2. Garment of Pharaoh that is upon my life; be removed by fire in the name of Jesus.

3. Thou power of impossibility in my destiny, die in the name of Jesus.

4. Let all impossibilities in my life become possible in the authority of the name of Jesus.

5. Every taskmaster assigned against me, I render you powerless in the name of Jesus.

6. I refuse to continue eating from the crumbs of the taskmaster's table.

7. All satanic agents assigned to prevent my freedom and prosperity I nullify your assignments, in the name of Jesus.

8. Heavenly Father, anoint me to recover the wasted years in every area of my life, in the name of Jesus.

9. O Sovereign Lord, I have fallen behind in many areas of my life. Empower me to recover all lost opportunities and wasted years, in the name of Jesus.

10. Any power that says I will not move forward in freedom and peace, be arrested by the blood of Jesus, in the name of Jesus.

11. Any power that wants to keep me in want in the midst of plenty, disappear by fire in the name of Jesus.

12. Any power that wants to draw me away from the presence of the Lord to distract me, loose your hold over my life, in the name of Jesus.

13. I declare by faith that I will get to my promised inheritance in the name of Jesus.

14. Any power that wants me to fulfill my destiny only partially, cursed be your assignment, in the name of Jesus.

15. O Lord my God, anoint me with power to destroy all unfavorable foundational covenants made by my ancestors on my behalf, in the name of Jesus.

16. O Lord my God, use my substance and virtue for the furtherance of the gospel, in the name of Jesus.

17. O Lord my God, arise and bless the portion of my inheritance in You, in the name of Jesus.

18. All my stolen virtues, be returned to me in the name of Jesus.

19. All my buried virtues, be exhumed in the name of Jesus.

20. Holy Spirit, reveal to me all ignorant ways in me, in the name of Jesus.

21. You my spirit man, from this day forth I charge you to refuse bewitchment, in the name of Jesus.

22. O Blood of Jesus, redeem my destiny in the authority of the name of Jesus.

23. All satanic weapons formed against my destiny, perish in the authority of the name of Jesus.

24. God's arrows of deliverance, locate my destiny in the name of Jesus.

25. All spiritual cobwebs cast over my destiny, be consumed by fire in the name of Jesus.

26. Let every gate opened in my life to the enemies of my soul be closed

27. Every strange fire burning against my destiny, quenched by the river of God in the name of Jesus.

28. Song: *God of deliverance, send down fire* (singing and clapping your hands for 15 minutes, sing a song of deliverance that has lyrics about God's consuming fire in it).

29. Every lid the enemy has put over my destiny; jump out in the name of Jesus.

30. Every serpent of captivity operating in my bloodline, stretch and die in the name of Jesus.

Session 4

THE DEAD BABY IS NOT YOURS

Scripture Reading: 1 Kings 3:27; Isaiah 22:19-25; Matthew 13:25

1 Kings 3:27 - So the king answered and said, "Give the first woman the living child, and by no means kill him; she is his mother."

A nd so was the king's ruling. And Solomon ruled by the wisdom of God. And so it shall be for you also, that any good thing that belongs to you, the enemy cannot trick you or confuse you into believing that what rightfully belongs to you is not yours. It should not be that someone should be empowered to separate you from your inheritance. It is your time to appeal through these prayers to the King of all righteousness and let Him rule in your favor. The dead child is not yours. I am excited about all the prayers in this book, but this session takes me to the edge of my seat each time I come to it. I believe God will perform a tremendous miracle of divine intervention for you as you pray this prayer with a contrite heart. Pray. You are now before the King, your lawgiver, your Righteous Judge. Believe that He will rule in your favor.

1. Every captive spirit caging my destiny, destroy yourself, in the name of Jesus.

2. Every power of darkness that followed my life and destiny up to this point, perish today, in the name of Jesus.

3. O power of the night assigned to steal my blessing "while men slept," disappear from my life, in the name of Jesus.

4. All evil associations that bring confusion, sorrow, frustration and misfortune into my life, be cut off from me by the sword of fire in the name of Jesus.

5. Any assembly of evildoers gathered against my well being, be roasted by the thunder and fire of God in the name of Jesus.

6. In the authority of the name of Jesus, O you lying lips opened against me, you will not prosper.

7. Blood of Jesus, redeem me from the works of all destiny stealers now, in the name of Jesus.

8. All satanic decisions taken against my progress are nullified in the name of Jesus.

9. Every spirit of deep sleep cast upon my spirit, soul and body, be lifted by the Arm of the Lord, in the name of Jesus.

10. O Lord my God, by your favor, promote me in the spiritual and in the natural, in the name of Jesus.

11. O Lord my God, open my spiritual eyes to see, in the name of Jesus.

12. Any satanic arrow fired against me, go back, locate and destroy your sender, in the name of Jesus.

13. Holy Ghost fire, arise and destroy the habitation and works of the wicked in my home, in the name of Jesus.

14. Holy Ghost fire, arise and destroy the habitation and works of the wicked in my life and calling, in the name of Jesus.

15. Holy Ghost fire, arise and destroy the habitation and works of the wicked in my finances, in the name of Jesus.

16. Holy Ghost fire, arise and destroy the habitation and works of the wicked in my career, in the name of Jesus.

17. Holy Ghost fire, arise and destroy the habitation and works of the wicked in my relationships, in the name of Jesus.

18. All network of unfriendly friends assigned to my life to embarrass me, be cut off from me now, in the name of Jesus.

19. In the name of Jesus, I declare that no power of darkness will switch my destiny.

20. All serpentine spirits spitting on my breakthrough, be roasted in the name of Jesus.

21. All enemies of the perfect will of God for my life, scatter into desolation in the name of Jesus.

22. Restore all superior friendships in my life that have been replaced with low friendships, in the name of Jesus.

23. All lines of low friendships falling upon my destiny are cut off in the name of Jesus.

24. I lift the banner of Jesus upon my destiny. Let fruitful friends that will enrich my life locate me, find me, and come to me now in the name of Jesus.

25. Let the anointing of joy and peace replace heaviness and sorrow in my life, in the name of Jesus.

26. Let abundance replace lack and insufficiency in my life, in the name of Jesus.

27. O Lord God, Spirit of all flesh, in the name of Jesus, give me a new inner man if I have been altered.

28. Holy Spirit, glorify Jesus in my life by activating the high call of God on my life.

29. I now receive grace and favor to prosper forever in the house of the Lord, in the name of Jesus.

30. Praise the Name of the Lord, for He is good and His mercy endures forever.

Session 5

REMOVING ALL EVIL PLANTINGS FROM YOUR LIFE

Scripture Reading: Matthew 15:13; Psalm 1

Matthew 15:13 But He answered and said, "Every plant which My heavenly Father has not planted will be uprooted.

Jesus says, "Every plant which My heavenly Father has not planted will be uprooted." Matthew 15:13. This means that for total deliverance and restoration to occur in someone's life, there are evil plantings, things that are present and growing in that person's life, contrary to the will of God for that person, that need to be uprooted first.

The purpose is this session is to confront, attack, and destroy evil plantings in all their forms so you can be free to fulfill your destiny in Jesus' name. Pray them aggressively, with focus and intensity. Victory is yours in Jesus' name.

1. What the enemy has programmed into my life to destroy me, O Lord remove it by fire in the name of Jesus.

   a) say the entire prayer point aloud three times; b) repeat the last portion of this prayer point for three minutes.

2. O Lord my God, remove whatever the enemy has planted in my life, in the name of Jesus.

3. Every good thing that the enemy has destroyed in my life, O Lord my God, restore it unto me this day in the name of Jesus.

4. Let my spiritual antenna be connected with the kingdom of God in the name of Jesus.

5. Every pollution in my spiritual life is purged with fire in the name of Jesus.

6. Holy Spirit, visit the dark room of my life, and destroy all unwanted materials in the name of Jesus.

7. Every wicked and stubborn spirit in my foundation, release me by fire and die, in the name of Jesus.

8. Every short-term and long-term project of the enemy in my life, be aborted in the name of Jesus.

9. All you organs of my body hear me, I charge you, and you will not cooperate with any enemy of my soul.

10. You organs of my body, receive the fire of sanctification in the name of Jesus.

11. Spirit of excellence, take control of my life in the name of Jesus.

12. Let the gift of revelation promote my life and destiny in the name of Jesus.

13. Holy Spirit, make your abode in me and let my life become signs and wonders in the name of Jesus.

14. Let the power of resurrection activate holiness and purity in me, in the name of Jesus.

15. Holy Ghost fire, arise and let every spiritual marriage conducted for me in the dream of the night, without my consent or knowledge, be destroyed in the name of Jesus

16. Any spiritual marriage that is destroying my holiness and purity, be dissolved in the name of Jesus.

17. Any spiritual marriage that is destroying my life and calling, be dissolved, in the name of Jesus.

18. Every power that has turned my life upside down is roasted by fire, in the name of Jesus.

19. O Lord my God, rearrange my destiny according to your plan, in the name of Jesus.

20. O Lord my God, crush every power that says I will not fulfill my destiny, in the name of Jesus.

21. O Lord my God, let every enemy of my life and calling be disgraced, in the name of Jesus.

22. Every evil network against my life and calling, be scattered, in the name of Jesus.

23. Every marine kingdom working against my progress and promotion, receive thunder in the name of Jesus.

24. Any power, spirit or personality removing good people out of my life, receive total confusion, in the name of Jesus.

25. O Lord my God, by your power gather all my divine helpers to me, in the name of Jesus.

26. O Lord my God, I beseech you by the mercies of heaven, scatter all conspiracy against my life and calling in the name of Jesus.

27. O Lord my God, let every contract spirit that comes before me that should not be allowed to come before you, be exposed, crippled, and fall to the ground in the name of Jesus.

28. Any power, spirit or personality using evil imagination against my life and calling, perish, in the name of Jesus.

29. Every power that has swallowed great opportunities from my life, vomit all my lost opportunities, in the name of Jesus.

30. Like a tree planted by the river, I declare that I bear fruit in my season in the name of Jesus.

Session 6

POSSESS YOUR POSSESSION

Scripture reading: Jeremiah 1:10; Job 31:35

Jeremiah 1:10 - See, I have this day set you over the nations and over the kingdoms, To root out and to pull down, To destroy and to throw down, To build and to plant."

Dearly beloved, it is time to pray. Oh yes, when you know that your glory is in captivity, when you know, that you know, that you know that you are capable of bringing in more but only less and less is coming your way, it is time to fight to possess your possession. When you know that it is your time to be celebrated, but only others are being celebrated and not you, when you know that your input is quality input but all you are getting is mediocre outcome, my friend, it is not normal, nor is it natural. When you know that all you do is hope and hope for the best, but when the time comes for your reward or promotion, you are jumped over in the queue, when you know that you know that you deserve better than you are doing now, my friend, you need to stand up and fight to possess your possession. It is a spiritual battle. I am here to tell you that your milk and honey is in the enemy's camp and it is time to engage the enemy of your soul in battle for the fulfillment of your destiny.

This battle is a six-stage fight. It is called: 1) Uproot; 2) Pull Down; 3) Destroy; 4) Throw down; 5) Build; 6) Plant.

In this fight, uproot; you will have to uproot. Pull down, you will have to pull things down that do not belong to your structure. Destroy; you will have to destroy the filthiness of the spirit from your surroundings. Throw down; you will have to throw down some unnecessary weight that has hindered you to this point before you get to your next level of promotion. All these you have to do before you build. All these you have to do before you plant. Once again, it is time to uproot, pull down, destroy, throw down, build, and plant. In doing so, you will be like a tree planted by the rivers of water.

1. All my glory under captivity is released to me in the name of Jesus.

2. I activate the divine authority inscribed into Jeremiah 1:10 upon my life, in the name of Jesus.

3. All that is mine shall be mine in the name of Jesus.

4. O Lord my God, let everything that the kingdoms of darkness have stolen from me be restored to me in the name of Jesus.

5. Every anti-Christ spirit assigned to downgrade my life and destiny, be arrested in the name of Jesus.

6. All spiritual thieves assigned to take my glory, receive the judgment of fire in the name of Jesus.

7. Spirit of non-accomplishment assigned to attack the work of my hands; I render you powerless in the name of Jesus.

8. Fire of revival to prosper in my season, explode in my life in the name of Jesus.

9. In the name of Jesus, I declare that I refuse to labor for another to harvest.

10. In the name of Jesus, I declare that I refuse to work for another to have the credit and the promotion.

11. Lord Jesus, commission twelve legions of your Father's angels to follow me wherever I go.

12. You satanic book of accusations against me, be destroyed by fire in the name of Jesus.

13. All sin and iniquity the enemy is using to weaken my bloodline, O Lord God of the spirit of all flesh, eradicate them from my bloodline in the name of Jesus.

14. Any evil arrow chasing my glory, backfire in the name of Jesus.

15. Any satanic material deposited upon my spirit man, be melted by fire in the name of Jesus.

16. Any satanic agent connecting me with contrary spirits is judged in the name of Jesus.

17. Any satanic agent sharing my glory with me is judged in the name of Jesus.

18. Any witchcraft mirror caging my progress is destroyed by thunder in the name of Jesus.

19. Every kingdom of darkness that says I will not fulfill my destiny and glory, I am the servant of the Most High God; therefore, I charge you to scatter totally in one hour, in the name of Jesus.

20. O enemy of my glory, be strangulated in the name of Jesus.

21. Let the power of my household enemies work against their own purposes, in the name of Jesus.

22. Any satanic agent in my foundation, using my glory for promotion, return my things back to me, in the name of Jesus.

23. You thunder of God, locate and scatter the habitation of the wicked in my foundation, in the name of Jesus.

24. All witchcraft visions and fleshly prophecies for my life are aborted in the name of Jesus.

25. O Arm of the Lord, declare total war against my enemies in the name of Jesus.

26. Whatsoever the enemy has deposited into my life, Holy Spirit, remove them now in the name of Jesus.

27. All those that the devil has anointed to oppose me, Holy Spirit, oppose them now in the name of Jesus.

28. Let the spirit of confusion locate my enemies and overcome them in the name of Jesus.

29. Any agents of darkness kindling strange fire against me, walk in your own fire, in the name of Jesus.

30. Let all my stolen kingdoms and their glories be restored to me in this season, in the name of Jesus.

Session 7

OPPRESSION IS NOT MY PORTION

Scripture reading: Daniel 7:12-18; Isaiah 26:13

Isaiah 26:13 - O LORD our God, masters besides You have had dominion over us; but by You only we make mention of Your name.

In today's fast-paced, fast result-oriented society, I often ask myself this question: "Why are we always thinking about and treating symptoms instead of causes?"

All you who are evangelists out there, who travel from city to city, you have probably heard these questions from well-meaning, born again believers when they come to pick you up at the airport once you land in their city: "Which spirit do you sense is ruling over our city?" "Which spirit is at work in our city?"

Many times, the believers who are asking these questions know the answer to their own questions, but they just want to hear it again. And in too many cases, the answer is oppression and depression.

Oppression and depression are the twin demonic spirits ruling over many cities or specific quadrants of many cities. My observation is that even though we have identified the culprit, we are still just fighting the symptoms, not the causes. Yes, we know that many lives are held captive by the spirits of oppression and depression, but how are we to deal with this? My humble spiritual remedy is to go to the root cause of the problem and attack the spirits behind feelings of gloominess that come upon people for no apparent reason.

There are several testimonies of believers who have prayed these prayers in our deliverance workshops across the nation, who came out of captivity. A particular woman in Ottawa, who had not laughed in four years, came to our meeting by accident. Halfway through the meeting, she began to sing for the first time in four years, and after the meeting she began to laugh, and volunteered to serve everybody the after-fellowship-snack. Her friends who had known her for over 20 years were amazed at how she was totally transformed within one hour.

These prayers will work for you. You are more than a conqueror through Christ Jesus.

1. Every wicked spirit sitting on my shoulder, receive fire from the mountain of God, in the name of Jesus.
2. Every serpent of darkness biting my destiny, stretch and die, in the name of Jesus.
3. Every seed of oppression in my life, dry up, in the name of Jesus.

4. Every spiritual bondage to debt and financial crisis in my life, be cut off in the name of Jesus.

5. Every oppression in my dream is smashed into pieces in the name of Jesus.

6. You yoke of backwardness in my life, be broken in the name of Jesus.

7. Holy Ghost fire, fight for me today in the name of Jesus.

8. Every serpent in the water attacking my life and calling, receive the salt of God and die, in the name of Jesus.

9. Owners of evil loads in my life, pick up your load and go in the name of Jesus.

10. In the name of Jesus, I charge you, you satanic program for my life and calling, you will not prosper.

11. Any attack of the enemy against the vision of God for my life and calling, scatter in the name of Jesus

12. Evil consultation against the program of God for my life and calling is nullified in the name of Jesus.

13. I declare that the mind that was in Christ Jesus is in me, and that oppression has no power over me.

14. Any river of oppression running into my life, dry up, in the name of Jesus.

15. You power of the heaviness assigned against my glory and calling, be destroyed by thunder, in the name of Jesus.

16. Every network of demons ragging against my life and calling, scatter in the name of Jesus.

17. Every spiritual gate closing against my life and calling is pulled down, in the name of Jesus.

18. You Jezebel spirit, killing God's prophets and practicing idolatry and witchcraft, sit no more on the circle of my life and calling. Fall and die, in the name of Jesus.

19. Any area of darkness in my life and calling, disappear, in the name of Jesus.

20. Every spiritual embargo against my glory and calling is lifted by thunder in the name of Jesus.

21. O Lord my God, open my inner eyes in the name of Jesus.

22. You Wisdom of God, make your abode in me, in the name of Jesus.

23. Lord Jesus, make your abode in me.

24. O Lord my God, hide me within the cleft your rock and make me untouchable for all my enemies, in the name of Jesus.

25. Any authority of darkness casting darkness upon my soul is overthrown in the name of Jesus.

26. O Light of God, shine forth upon my soul in the name of Jesus.

27. O my soul, receive strength and come out of captivity, in the name of Jesus.

28. Lord Jesus, let my glory glorify you.

29. Let the mantle and the anointing to receive brightness in my soul fall upon me, in the name of Jesus.

30. I am free in the mighty name of Jesus.

Session 8

SPEAK TO YOUR MOUNTAINS

Scripture Reading: Psalm 68; Psalm 107:23-24; Psalm 42:7; Psalm 36:8; I Peter 3:19; Psalm 142:7; Amos 2:6; Job 20:15; Psalm 97:3; Psalm 118:8-10; Zechariah 4:7

Amos 2:6 - Thus says the LORD: "For three transgressions of Israel, and for four, I will not turn away its punishment, because they sell the righteous for silver, and the poor for a pair of sandals.

There is a deep secret here. Open your spirit to receive it. First you have to learn to speak to your mountain. How? Look at the mountain face to face as if it were a human standing in front of you, and speak. This is one of the many unused prayer secrets in the Scriptures. Remember Moses? Moses the man whom God himself respects so much that he, the Sovereign God, wouldn't even mention his name without the affectionate title, "My servant Moses"? Yes, Moses was told to speak to the rock and watch the miracle happen. God did not say, "Pray for me to do something about the water crisis." He said, "Speak to the rock." He is giving you the authority today to do something about your mountain or your crisis. How? Take a cue from Zechariah 4:7

Zechariah 4:7 — who are you, O great mountain? Before Zerubbabel you shall become level ground! And he shall bring forth the cap-stone with shouts of "Grace, grace to it!"

Go for it. Speak to your mountains. Victory is yours in the mighty name of our Lord Jesus. You are more than a conqueror in Christ Jesus.

1. Holy Ghost, arise and destroy every evil habitation in me, in Jesus' name.
2. Every satanic incantation pronounced against me, be rendered null and void, in Jesus' name.
3. Holy Ghost, arise in your power and wage war against my adversaries in Jesus' name.
4. All you serpents of the sea, I command you in Jesus' name to vomit everything you have swallowed up in my life.
5. Holy Ghost, in the name of Jesus, show me where the enemy has kept or buried my blessings.
6. Holy Ghost, in the authority of the name of Jesus, arise, locate and destroy the stronghold of the powers of darkness that are taking my blessings captive.

7. Holy Ghost, in the name of Jesus, arise and chase away every spiritual dog pursing my destiny.

8. Every power of darkness transacting business underneath great waters, release my virtues, blessings, glory, destiny and calling in Jesus' name.

9. O my spirit, come out of every satanic prison, in Jesus' name.

10. O Lord God, arise and set my spirit free from satanic prison, in the name of Jesus.

11. Raising your right hand to heaven, declare the following: I register my life for progress in Jesus' name.

12. Every demonic transaction going on contrary to the will of God for my life, be silenced and be terminated in the name of Jesus.

13. Any satanic agents that have swallowed my glory and honor, vomit my glory and benefit by thunder, in the name Jesus.

14. O Lord my God, let fire go before you and destroy all your enemies and all of mine, in the name of Jesus.

15. Every stranger around me, remove them in the name of Jesus. (Say numbers 15 and 16 before leaving home for a job interview, performance review, or an important meeting).

16. With your right hand over your head, declare the following: Power of promotion, rest upon me, in the name of Jesus.

17. Let all flesh and demons be silenced before God now. Speak, O Lord, Your servant is hearing.

18. Pause for five to 15 minutes or more, then declare the following:

19. I connect with the power and authority of the Ancient of Days, in Jesus' name.

20. I connect with the branch and the root of Jesse (Isaiah 11:1-3), in the name of Jesus.

21. I connect with the anointing of fire and power on the day of Pentecost, in the name of Jesus.

22. I connect with the anointing of divine authority without measure in the name of Jesus.

23. I receive the anointing to be fruitful and multiply in the name of Jesus

24. I connect with the anointing grace and favor in the name of Jesus.

25. I connect with the anointing of ease and good things coming to me easily from this day forth, in the name of Jesus.

26. I connect with the anointing of the tree planted by the rivers of water to prosper in my season, in the name of Jesus.

27. I connect with the anointing of increased faith to move mountains in the name of Jesus.

28. I connect with the anointing to have my land yield its increase, in the name of Jesus.

29. I connect with the anointing to know and attract my divine helpers, in the name of Jesus.

30. I connect with the anointing to know my hour of visitation in the name of Jesus.

Session 9

O MY SOUL, I COMMAND YOU TO COME OUT OF PRISON

Scripture Reading: Amos 2:6; Psalm 129; Isaiah 42:22; Isaiah 61:1; Luke 4:18-19

Isaiah 42:22 - But this is a people robbed and plundered; all of them are snared in holes, and they are hidden in prison houses; they are for prey, and no one delivers; for plunder, and no one says, "Restore!"

Are you ready for a challenge? Are you going through something that looks so strange, so unusual, that it defies human understanding? It is time to pray to release your soul, your well being, and your virtues from captivity. If you are in a prison, it means there is a strange master ruling over your life. For someone to be put into prison, there has to be a master ruling over someone, in which the master has power.

If you believe it is your time to come out of captivity and live in freedom in Christ, then it is time to stand against strange kings ruling over your life. The spiritual problem of souls in captivity is so pertinent that in Psalm 142:7, David screamed out to God, "Bring my soul out of prison, that I may praise Your name." Anyone, including spiritual authorities who have power over you, can do anything they want with you, including selling you into captivity or servitude.

For you to be sold, there has to be someone with power over you to sell you. You know you are under this type of captivity when you, the superior, find yourself serving your subordinates, and you, the learned and accomplished, find yourself at the end of the list when it is time to celebrate accomplished people. It is time to pray, brethren. Luke 4:18-19 records that Jesus, when he went to the synagogue in Nazareth in the day of Sabbath, declared that he came to set the captives free. Indeed, Jesus alone has the power to set you free. Now, stand up for your freedom. Pray.

1. Every evil cord of wickedness, sin or iniquity blocking my communication with heaven and God, be cut off in the name of Jesus.

2. My life is not for sale. I refuse to be sold by any demon power, in the name of Jesus.

3. Every power, spirit or personality listening to my prayers in order to report them to the demonic world, receive deafness in the name of Jesus.

4. Heavenly Father, expose and destroy the workers of iniquity assigned to downgrade my destiny, in Jesus' name.

5. O heavens, I charge you to fight for me today, in the name of Jesus.

6. Any power diverting the will of God out of my life is cut off from my life and destiny, in the name of Jesus.

7. O Lord, arise and let every line of darkness that has fallen upon my life be cut off in the name of Jesus.

8. I declare victory over all powers attacking my glory and calling, in the name of Jesus.

9. Holy Spirit, activate the will of God in my life and calling, in the name of Jesus.

10. By my words, let the will of my enemies against me backfire, in the name of Jesus.

11. Every plot of the enemy against me is dissolved in the name of Jesus.

12. By my words, I command the confidence of my enemies to be dashed into pieces, in the name of Jesus.

13. Any power of darkness creating crises of identification and lack of confidence in my life is removed, in the name of Jesus.

14. Every spiritual manipulation against my glory and calling shall be a total failure, in the name of Jesus.

15. All those who are bent to destroy my personality are disarmed, in the name of Jesus.

16. O Lord, vindicate my life and calling in the name of Jesus.

17. O Lord, reveal to me what you have called me to be in life, in the name of Jesus.

18. Every strange god assigned to attack my destiny, personality, glory, and calling, attack your sender, in the name of Jesus.

19. O Ark of God, pursue every Dagon assigned against me, in the name of Jesus.

20. Let the hosts of heaven pursue all those enraged against me, in the name of Jesus.

21. Let the Ark of the Lord come into my house today, to locate and fight the power of the opposition against me, in the name of Jesus.

22. O Ark of the Lord, wherever I have been accepted in the past and they are now refusing me, arise and fight for me in the name of Jesus.

23. O Ark of the Lord, wherever I have been rejected in the past, let my spirit man be accepted now, in the name of Jesus.

24. O Lion of Judah, devour every opposition raging against me now, in the name of Jesus.

25. I refuse to be sold for a pair of shoes or for silver, in the name of Jesus.

26. I resist and refuse any sale of my glory and calling, in the name of Jesus.

27. Holy Spirit, in the name of Jesus, reveal to me areas of my life where strange masters are ruling over my life. Increase me, O Lord, so your name may be glorified.

28. Pause for five to 15 minutes or more, with eyes closed.

29. I receive strength and anointing to come out of captivity in the name of Jesus.

30. It is written concerning me that my "land shall not be sold permanently," therefore I command you, O my soul, to come out of captivity, in the authority of the name of Jesus.

Session 10

LET ALL ROADBLOCKS BE REMOVED

Scripture Reading: Amos 2:8; Psalm 124

Amos 2:8 - They lie down by every altar on clothes taken in pledge, and drink the wine of the condemned in the house of their god.

Pray these prayers if victory is always eluding you when you come close to it., Do you feel you have been made to start over just when you felt your life and plans moving upward? Has this happened to you not one time, but on more than one occasion?. If you live in a situation where bad words are being spread all over concerning you, it does not matter if these words are true or not. It is important that these bad words are removed from circulation in the spirit world and that the favor of God is restored upon your life. What is most important is that you need to stand against the powers that are condemning you and have put you in the box of the "condemned." Let's pray.

1. I decree now that the wine of the condemned drunk against me become a poison for my enemies, in the name of Jesus.

2. O wine of condemnation drunk against me, I nullify your intended expectations over my life, in the name of Jesus.

3. O Lord my God, let the mighty among my enemies flee away from me naked, in the name of Jesus.

4. I declare that I am innocent of all great transgressions. The blood of Jesus has paid for all my iniquities; therefore I am cleared and cleansed from all accusations of the wicked ones against me, in the name of Jesus.

5. Every power of darkness that has arrested my life and calling, release me now in the name of Jesus.

6. Every word of malicious gossip in circulation against me is now withdrawn from circulation, in the name of Jesus.

7. Every voice rising against me in the spirit world is silenced in the name of Jesus.

8. Every association of demons cooperating with workers of iniquity from my father's house is shattered into desolation, in the name of Jesus.

9. O vehicle of my destiny, be repaired and put back on the road, in the name of Jesus.

10. Holy Spirit, arise and send me divine help, in the name of Jesus.

11. All roadblocks and impediments to the fulfillment of my life and calling are removed in Jesus' name.

12. You yoke of frustration, failure and non-fulfillment over my life, be destroyed by fire in the name of Jesus.

13. You siege of the wicked over my life, be lifted by the Arm of the Lord in the name of Jesus.

14. You rod of discouragement cast upon my progress, I smite you in the name of Jesus.

15. You rod of disappointment cast upon my purposes, wither in the name of Jesus.

16. A reservoir of blessing is our God. O Lord my God, pour blessings upon me now from your reservoir of blessings and power, in the name of Jesus.

17. Holy Spirit arise and activate my ministry and calling in the name of Jesus.

18. O Lord my God, let every word I have spoken against my life be reversed, in the name of Jesus.

19. My God is the God of the living, therefore He will answer me in the name of Jesus.

20. Every prince of this world opposing me is overthrown in the name of Jesus.

21. Every prince of this world reigning over my life, I cast you out in the name of Jesus.

22. Any strange power or personality living with me in my house, receive fire of destruction in the name of Jesus.

23. Any stranger and agent of the enemy of my soul operating within my circle of friendship, be exposed and be cast out in the name of Jesus.

24. Every satanic agent erecting evil altars above or around me, receive total confusion, in the name of Jesus (This prayer is suitable for those living in multiple unit homes, apartments or multiple household buildings).

25. Every demonic authority in my environment operating against me is arrested by the blood of Jesus and the power of the Holy Ghost, in the name of Jesus.

26. I receive deliverance from evil powers and demonic authorities controlling my purpose and destiny, in the name of Jesus.

27. Song: *I want the fire that is fresh, old fire cannot do it.* Sing this song if you know it. If not, sing a fire song similar to it.

28. Any part of my body or organ that is stolen, be returned to me by fire, in the name of Jesus.

29. Song: *The Lord reigneth, let the earth tremble.* Sing this song if you know it. If not, sing a song similar to it.

30. I proclaim that the shout of Hallelujah will not cease in my life, in the name of Jesus.

O FIRE OF GOD, PURSUE MY PURSUERS

Scripture Reading: Psalm 18:37; Psalm 35:3; Exodus 15:9; I Samuel 30:8; II Chronicles 14:13; Psalm 83:5

Psalm 18:37 - I have pursued my enemies and overtaken them; neither did I turn back again till they were destroyed.

If you've spent your life up to this point running from an enemy who is bent on destroying you, there comes a time when you have to say, "Enough is enough." That time has come. That time is now. Whatever the evil power is that is pursuing you, for whatever reason, now is your time for a shift in power. It is time for your soul to be refreshed in the power of His might. Receive power to pursue your pursuers.

1.   Every demon assigned to arrest me from my foundation, be arrested in the name of Jesus.

2. O Lord my God, empty all enemies of my soul and let them be desolate, in the name of Jesus.

3. Every power that has vowed that I will not excel in life, I render you powerless, in the name of Jesus.

4. I command the elements of nature to fight all enemies of my life and calling, in the name of Jesus.

5. Let the blood of Jesus, mixed with the fire of God, pursue all enemies of my life and calling, in the name of Jesus.

6. I declare that my destiny will not lay dormant, but activated to the glory of God, in the name of Jesus.

7. Every spiritual horn fighting my destiny, perish in the name of Jesus.

8. Any power assigned to oppose my destiny, O Holy Ghost fire, oppose them in the name of Jesus.

9. Mountains of difficulties before me are melted by fire in the mighty name of Jesus.

10. Every secret agent around me, operating against my destiny, is exposed and rendered powerless, in the name of Jesus.

11. Every evil farmer planting evil seed into my life, harvest your evil, in the name of Jesus.

12. Every evil leg roaming around against me is paralyzed in the name of Jesus.

13. O Lord my God, let the kingdom of darkness be confused because of me, in the name of Jesus.

14. All satanic artilleries operating against me are bulldozed by thunder in the name of Jesus.

15. You strongman in my foundation, be slain in the name of Jesus.

16. Every power that destroyed my ancestors, in the name of Jesus, I adjure that you will not destroy me.

17. Every power that destroyed my ancestors, I receive power to destroy you in the name of Jesus.

18. You, my inner man, hear me; you will not destroy my outer man. (Your inner man is your personality; your outer man is what people see.)

19. Holy Spirit, let the ministry of angels flow continually in my life and ministry in the name of Jesus.

20. O Lord my God, let every indwelling sin in me be uprooted in the name of Jesus.

21. You destiny diverters, I declare that you will not have dominion over my life, in the name of Jesus.

22. O Light of God, shine forth upon my life and calling, in the name of Jesus.

23. O Lord my God, raise your standard against my pursuers in the name of Jesus.

24. My inner eye receives light in the name of Jesus.

25. My inner man receives divine strength in the name of Jesus

26. Every power from my father's house that says I will not reach my potential, fall and die, in the name of Jesus.

27. Any power from my father's house that is delaying the manifestation of my glory, fall and die in the name of Jesus.

28. All contrary spirits from my place of birth (or place of origin) that is delaying my glory and enthronement, fall and die in the name of Jesus.

29. Holy Ghost fire, pursue my pursuers, in the name of Jesus.

30. My soul is surrounded by the love of God, in the name of Jesus.

FOR MARRIAGE-MINDED CHRISTIAN SINGLES - ON RECEIVING THEIR MATE FROM GOD

D earest friend,
A word of wisdom for you.

I want you to know that there three kinds of mates out there for you: 1) the one you choose for yourself; 2) the one the devil will send your way; 3) the one God has had for you before the foundation of the earth was laid.

My prayer is that your spiritual eyesight is open for you to see and settle only for the third one.

Scripture Reading: Genesis 1:27-28; Genesis 2:18; Genesis 2:21-24

Genesis 2:18 - And the LORD God said, "It is not good that man should be alone; I will make him a helper comparable to him."

1. O Blood of Jesus, remove all impediments to my marital fulfillment, in the name of Jesus.

2. (For men), O you woman whom God has ordained for my marital fulfillment, be fulfilled now in the name of Jesus.

3. (For women) O you man whom God has ordained for my marital fulfillment, be fulfilled now in the name of Jesus.

4. All bondage, blockage, and limitation to my marital fulfillment, be removed by fire in the name of Jesus.

5. O God of wonders, give me a glorious vision of marital fulfillment, in the name of Jesus.

6. Favor of God, arrange all things for me now, in the name of Jesus.

7. Arise, O Lord, and place judgment on principalities, marine powers, and territorial spirits working against my marital fulfillment, in the name of Jesus.

8. Any spirit, power, personality, principality, and evil expectation raging against my marital breakthrough, be quenched by fire in the name of the Lord Jesus.

9. (For men) O Lord God of the spirit of all flesh, wherever my God-ordained wife is now in the world, bring her to me by your zeal, in the name of Jesus!

10. (For women) O Lord God of the spirit of all flesh, wherever my God-ordained husband is now in the world, bring him to me by your zeal, in the name of Jesus!

11. Pray in tongues for 15 minutes.

12. Move on to the special divine matchmaker prayer below.

ANOINTED PRAYER FOR MARRIAGE-MINDED CHRISTIAN MEN

Instruction:

Pray this prayer three times daily until you find the bone of your bones, the flesh of your flesh, and the woman of your life.

First, pray this prayer by reading it aloud, standing by your bedside before going to bed. Let it be the last thing you do before going to bed. Do well by not engaging in any other activity after this prayer; i.e., TV, phone, or other distractions before bed. By praying this prayer before going to bed, you will receive divine revelations with respect to the one who is your promised bride.

Second, pray this prayer just upon getting up from bed. Stand and read this prayer aloud from your bedside. This will open your spiritual eyesight to recognize your true wife, your promised bride, when you see her. If she is already in your life, the light will come on and you will recognize her.

Third, stand and read this prayer aloud between noon and 3:00 p.m. This will remove all satanic technologies activated against you during the waking hours, clearing the way for you to receive your godly wife.

Dear Heavenly Father:

In the precious name of my Lord Jesus Christ, I come to you to declare that I stand in the gap for myself to resist any plan and attempt of Satan to hinder or delay the coming of my promised bride. It is written, "... resist the devil and he will flee from you." Therefore, I resist any plan of Satan to gain ground in this battle for my wife. In the name of my Lord Jesus, I put a stop to Satan's work against me in every area of my life: my finances, my ministry, my family, my wife-to-be, my academic life, my social life, my businesses, my health, my upward mobility, and in every department of my life.

I call upon the power in the blood of the Lord Jesus to break all spiritual ties, all sexual ties, all soul ties (known or unknown) and all hindering spirits and the spiritual forces of darkness frustrating my marital life. I cancel all incantations, all active prayers, all carnal prophecies, and all spiritual principles working against me and my marital fulfillment. In the name of my Lord Jesus, I also cancel the spiritual powers invested in such prayers and spiritual activities.

In the name of my Lord Jesus, I resist all spiritual forces of darkness that are hindering or delaying the coming of my wife. I resist any spiritual blindness cast upon me to prevent me from recognizing my beloved wife. As the spiritual watchman of the Lord Most High, I declare that I allow only those things that are ordained by God's Holy Spirit to be active in my life. I reject anything in me that will hinder or delay the coming of my wife. I declare further that only my promised bride will come to me and be revealed to me. I declare that the counterfeit wife is not my portion in the Lord, and that her way to me will be dark and slippery, in the name of Jesus.

Heavenly Father, I pray that you will not allow your purposes for my marital life to be thwarted by the enemies of my soul. I make a matter of record and declare that Jesus is the Lord of my life and that no strange king, such as the king of celibacy, will rule over my life. I therefore call on you, O Ancient of Days, to rise as a man of war and fight on my behalf for the redemption of my marital life from the hands of the king of celibacy. Remember me, O Lord, and do not be silent. Act speedily, O Lord God of Mount Zion. Arise, O Lord, and let your enemies be scattered, in the name of my Lord Jesus.

O God of wonders, I ask you to remember the covenant that Jesus made on the cross through his death that brought the victory over the powers of darkness. I claim that victory now for the immediate release of my wife. I legislate in the heavens now the release of my wife, in the name of my Lord Jesus. Righteous Father, I bring the power of the cross, the sacrifice of the Lord Jesus now into effect in this situation.

In the matters of my true wife from God, I hereby cancel any argument against me in the spirit world, and thereby renounce any covenants or spiritual marriage made by me or on my behalf. Let all covenants signed against me in the air, on the land, in the sea, on the field, underneath the earth, underneath great waters, on the phone, in the mail, on crossroads, in any vehicle of transportation, in any dwelling place of man, beast or spirits in the dark or in the day, with the new moon, with any heavenly bodies, or with spiritual forces of darkness at home and abroad, be now cancelled by the blood of my Lord Jesus, in the name of the Lord Jesus.

I now ask the Lord of Hosts to release the angels of the Living God to fight on my behalf to secure the arrival of my true wife, a woman of virtue, of understanding, and of good countenance, the bone of my bones and flesh of my flesh, according to your perfect will for my life.

Hear me, O ye heavens, hear me, O ye earth. It is written: "touch not my anointed, do my prophet no harm." Therefore now, all you anti-marriage spirits, powers, and personalities militating against my marital fulfillment, release me now and let me go find my help-meet, in the authority of the name of Jesus.

I lift your name up, Lord Jesus, as a banner over my life. Let the trumpets sound! May the peoples know that you are the Lord. You are the only name I know, O Lord Jesus. Thank you, Lord, for my wife. In Jesus' name I pray. Amen!

ANOINTED PRAYER FOR MARRIAGE-MINDED CHRISTIAN WOMEN

Instruction:

Pray this prayer three times daily until the man God has ordained for you from before the foundation of the earth was laid finds you.

You are a good thing to be found, for it is written, "He who finds a wife, finds a good thing."

First, pray this prayer by reading it aloud, kneeling by your bedside before going to bed. Let it be the last thing you do before going to bed. Do well by not engaging in any other activity after this prayer; i.e., TV, phone, or other distractions before going to bed.

Second, pray this prayer just upon getting up from bed. Stand and read this prayer aloud in your bathroom.

Third, stand and read this prayer aloud between noon and 3:00 p.m. three times a week, preferably Friday, Saturday and Sunday. Pray this section from or out of your kitchen.

Dear Heavenly Father:

In the precious name of my Lord Jesus Christ, I come to you to declare that I stand in the gap for my marital destiny to resist any plan of Satan to prevent the man of my life from finding me. It is written, "… resist the devil and he will flee from you." Therefore, I resist any plan of Satan to gain ground in this battle for my life.

In the name of my Lord Jesus, I put a stop to Satan's work against me in every area of my life. I call upon the power in the blood of the Lord Jesus to break all spiritual ties, all sexual ties, all soul ties (known or unknown), all inordinate affections, and all hindering spirits and the spiritual forces of darkness frustrating my marital life. I cancel all active prayers, all carnal prophecies, and all spiritual principles working against me and my marital fulfillment. In the name of my Lord Jesus, I also cancel the spiritual powers invested in such prayers and spiritual activities.

In the name of my Lord Jesus, I resist all spiritual forces of darkness that are hindering or delaying the coming of my true husband, the one out of whom I came. I resist any spiritual blindness cast upon me to prevent me recognizing my beloved husband. I reject anything in me that will hinder or delay the coming of my beloved husband. I declare further that only my promised husband will come to me and be revealed to me. I declare that the counterfeit husband is not my portion in the Lord.

Heavenly Father, I pray that you will not allow your purposes for my marital life to be thwarted by the enemies of my soul. I make a matter of record and declare that Jesus is the Lord of my life and that no strange king, such as the king of celibacy, will rule over my life. I therefore call on you, O Ancient of Days, to rise as a man of war and fight on my behalf for the redemption of my marital life from the hands of the king of celibacy. Remember me, O Lord, and do not be silent. Act speedily, O Lord God of Mount Zion. Arise,

O Lord, and let your enemies be scattered in the name of my Lord Jesus.

O God of wonders, I ask you to remember the covenant that Jesus made on the cross through His death that brought the victory over the powers of darkness. I claim that victory now for the immediate release of my husband. I legislate in the heavens now the release of my husband, in the name of my Lord Jesus. Righteous Father, I bring the power of the cross, the sacrifice of the Lord Jesus now into effect in this situation.

In the matters of my true husband from God, I hereby cancel any argument against me in the spirit world and thereby renounce any covenants or spiritual marriage made by me or on my behalf. Let all covenants signed against me in the air, on the land, in the sea, on the field, underneath the earth, underneath great waters, on the phone, in the mail, on crossroads, in any vehicle of transportation, in any dwelling place of man, beasts or spirits, in the dark or in the day, with the new moon, with any heavenly bodies, or with spiritual forces of darkness at home and abroad, be now cancelled by the blood of my Lord Jesus, in the name of the Lord Jesus.

I now ask the Lord of Hosts to release the angels of the Living God to fight on my behalf to secure the arrival of my true husband, according to your perfect will for my life. Hear me, O ye heavens, hear me O ye earth. It is written: "touch not my anointed, do my prophet no harm" Therefore now, all you anti-marriage spirits, powers, and personalities militating against my marital fulfillment, release me now and let me go and become a gift of God for the one who is looking for me, in the authority of the name of Jesus.

I lift your name up, Lord Jesus, as a banner over my life. Let the trumpet sound! May the peoples know that you are the Lord. You are the only name I know, O Lord Jesus. Thank you, Lord, for my husband. In Jesus' name I pray. Amen!

Part Two

Preface

Dear friends, it is my faith and assurance that these prayers will be extremely beneficial in preparing you to receive a miracle from God. *Yes*, these prayers will open the door to miracles for you in every area of your life! You will become a *living testimony* as everyone around you asks, "How did it happen?" and your answer will be, "It is marvelous in our sight *because* it is the Lord's doing!"

Whether you are a person in need of deliverance or a minister of deliverance, we are pleased to make these anointed prayers available to you as a tool of deliverance, either for yourself or in ministry to someone else. As you use them with *"great expectation,"* **you shall receive** *"great deliverance"* in the Name of our Lord Jesus Christ!

Joseph A. Dodjro

God's servant and yours

Introduction

Dear friend:

Which activities are included in your spiritual routine? Which spiritual exercises have taken root in your daily life? Reading, studying and meditating upon the Word? Praying? Which daily scriptures do you read? Or do you have a daily routine of specific scriptures you read daily? Regardless of whichever activity is present in your daily spirituality, we encourage you to add this prayer manual to your daily routine, and we believe in doing so, and by faith in Jesus Christ and your aggressively praying these prayers, success will be yours in all your endeavors.

It is my faith and assurance that these prayers will be extremely beneficial in preparing you to receive a miracle from God. *Yes*, these prayers will open the door to miracles for you in every area of your life! You will become a *living testimony* as everyone around you asks, "How did it happen?" and your answer will be, "It is marvelous in our sight *because* it is the Lord's doing!"

Whether you are a person in need of deliverance or a deliverance minister, we believe God that these anointed prayers will work for you as a tool of deliverance, either for yourself or in ministry to someone else. As you use them with great expectation, you shall receive great deliverance in the Name of our Lord Jesus Christ!

The Bible talks about the sons of Issachar in I Chronicles 7:5, referring to them not only as mighty men of valor, but also in I Chronicles 12:32 as having "understanding of the times, to know what Israel ought to do..."

We ought to know our times. We ought to see the onslaught of the enemy in our generations, attacking every aspect of our lives, and get filled with holy indignation and do something about it. And as Christians, doing something about it ought to include getting your spiritual warfare prayer mode in order to change the status in our life and the lives of thousands of others. It is your time to pray. Go ahead. Pray.

Make these proclamations aloud:

Send Now Prosperity, O Lord!

F or success and prosperity to occur in someone else, two things have to happen:

First, all reproach and contempt have to be removed.

Second, the grace, favor, and mercy of God have to be activated upon the person's life.

This is a two-fold spiritual transaction. It is a divine intervention that causes the garment of reproach and contempt to be removed from someone's life. If this garment, which is a garment of disfavor, is not removed, even if you are promoted to your next position of entitlement, everyone will start finding fault in your action. However the garment of disfavor is removed, and grace, mercy, and favor are activated upon your life, everyone will start saying great, sweet and endearing things about you. The sign that grace, favor and mercy are activated upon someone's life is that the person will say something so simple and people will start getting excited, as if that was the first time anyone ever said it. But the same statement, someone else will say it, and there will be no reaction. That means there is grace on the first person.

Let's pray.

All powers of darkness competing against my destiny, comfort and well being, be scattered into desolation, in the name of Jesus. Every organized network of the underworld and their demonic cohorts assigned to oppose me, be disorganized in the name of Jesus. Arise, O east wind of the Lord! Arise in your strength, locate and blast out every contrary power delaying the fulfillment of my destiny; dislodge every principality sitting on my blessings, in the name of Jesus. O zeal of the Lord, arise and perform a miracle for me at this hour in the name of Jesus. O arm of the Lord, arise and hold back every hand of the enemy stretched out against me. All powers of darkness standing at the gate of my promised land, be consumed by fire from the Lord. Controlling hereditary spirits assigned to intercept my good fortune, be destroyed in the name of Jesus. I sprinkle the blood of Jesus over all stubborn issues in my life, and I release divine solution over them all, for total protection. Holy Spirit, be my counselor in every department of my life, day and night. I declare that neither the devil nor my flesh will win this battle, for my weapons are mighty in God for the pulling down of strongholds of the enemy. Let every stumbling block placed before me be removed from my way, in the name of Jesus. All evil altars speaking against my prosperity, be pulled down by fire in the name of Jesus. Oh zeal of the Lord, empower me to build, strengthen, and exalt the horns of the altar of the Lord in my life, in the name of Jesus. You spirit of devourer assigned against my handiwork, be judged with burning judgment, in the name of the Lord Jesus. You devourer operating in my finances, the Lord rebuke you. O Captain of the Lord's army, surround me with the shield of victory for this battle, for my prosperity in all areas of my life. O mighty, rushing wind from heaven, surround us with the shield of Pentecost, in the name of Jesus. You counsel and works of the wicked against the call of God in my life, I call the thunder of God upon you and your hosts, in the name of Jesus. I call heaven and earth as a witness against you today, you counsel of the ungodly against me ~ *be judged in the name of Jesus*. You evil altar erected against me, the outstretched arm of God is against you. All satanic warrants issued to arrest me or my property, arrest the warrant officer in the name of Jesus. All satanic inspectors patrolling around to catch me or my property, catch the patrol officer in the name of Jesus. All evil agents monitoring my life and the way to my prosperity, receive total confusion. All my certificates, diplomas, degrees, designations, recognitions, awards and rewards held by powers of darkness, be released to me at once in the name of Jesus. All satanic agents who are invoking the dead to obtain information to harm me, be cut off, in the name of Jesus. All unwanted visitors in my home, vacate by fire in the name of Jesus. Lord, connect me with people and friends in high places, in the name of Jesus. O mighty I Am that I Am, move me forward through supernatural promotion in the name of Jesus. Holy Spirit, investigate all circumstances in my life and let everything that is abnormal and substandard in my life become normal and according to our standards, in the name of Jesus. Every power of darkness challenging the authority of God in my life, be shattered into deso-lation in the name of Jesus. There is none like You, O Lord, Mighty One of Jacob ~ *I praise You!* In Jesus' name I've prayed. Amen.

Fighting with the Sword
of your Mouth

I take my position in heavenly places in Christ Jesus at the right hand of God, and I declare that my Heavenly Father is about to bless me! Now, you blocking spirit and evil followers, depart from me, in the name of Jesus. All workers of iniquity surrounding me, I break your bonds in pieces and cast away your cords from me. Satan, you have had your chance and time to parade your choices and unwholesome options before me. Now is the time to move out of the way, for God to bring His choices to me, in the Name of Lord. Let my head and my glory arise in the name of Jesus. Let the anointing that caused Aaron's rod to bud fall upon me. Let the plans of the enemies of my soul be exposed and let the cords break that tie me down. Let every satanic watch set against my destiny break into irreparable pieces. Let every satanic clock set to work contrary to my glory collapse by thunder in the name of Jesus. Let the storeroom of the Lord be opened for me this season, to receive my promotion from the Sovereign Lord. Let the siege of the enemy over my destiny be lifted at once by angelic intervention. All you spiritual giants opposing my promotion, I smite you with the sword of fire, in the name of Jesus. O Lord, prosper me during the reign of (insert the name of your local politicians of all levels of government – local, regional, national) in the name of Jesus.

This is Your Day of New Beginnings of Promotion

O Sovereign Lord, it is written in your Word that the time to favor Zion is now. Therefore, I declare that it is time for God to release bountiful increase into my life, in Jesus' name. In Jesus' name, O Lord God of Hosts, I beseech you by the mercies of heaven to look down from heaven and visit this vine, the vineyard of your Right Hand. O Lord, let your hand be upon the man of your Right Hand, in Jesus' mighty name. O Lord my God, let your hand be upon the son of man whom you made strong for yourself. Lord, connect me with rulers of this world, men and women in high places, for the fulfillment of my destiny, in the name of Jesus. Holy Spirit, direct me to be at the right place at the right time in this season. By your hand, O Lord, bring the mastermind group of your choice into my life, for the benefit of your kingdom. Spirit of the Living God, bring into my life the best of men and women, who will add value to my life. O Lord, remove from my circle of friendship and acquaintances Satan's agents whose assignment is to take away from me without adding anything. Oh Jehovah Elohim, breathe the Breath of Life upon my life and let all unfulfilled longings of my heart be fulfilled at once. I declare by faith that I am marked for success by the Holy Spirit for God. I am marked for the position of prominent citizenship and am a respected member of the community, in the name of Jesus. Let heaven and earth come together and work in unison now for the immediate release of my promotion, in the name of Jesus. Thank you, Lord Jesus, for elevating my destiny.

Evicting Demonic Intruders

O Lord God of Elijah, as I embark upon this operation, let your fire enter my bones in the name of Jesus. Any evil presence in this vicinity and/or in my body, disappear at the going forth of these words: *Receive thunder in the name of Jesus!* You satanic fighter opposing me, what are you waiting for? Fall and die by burning judgment, in the name of Jesus. All spiritual cages that have been designed for my life, be destroyed by fire in the name of Jesus. O Lord, send down your fire and shut it up in my bones in the name of Jesus. O fire of God, be shut up in my bones and make me a moving target for the enemies of my soul. Every satanic contamination in my life, be expelled by fire in the name of Jesus. O Lord God of Sinai, turn my weaknesses to strength in the name of Jesus. All satanic praise singers assigned to my life, be silenced in the name of Jesus. (i.e., I know that the song writers say that Saul killed his thousands and David killed his tens of thousands, but I don't want to hear it.) Therefore, all you satanic praise singers in the day of my victory, be silenced. Every witchcraft attack upon my life and destiny, be cancelled in the name of Jesus. Every witchcraft manipulation of my life and calling, die in the name of Jesus. Every evil distraction assigned to my life, be removed by fire in the name of Jesus. Every evil hindrance to my calling, be removed by angelic intervention, in the name of Jesus. Every witchcraft arrow of non-achievement in my life, go back to your sender, in the name of Jesus. Every ancestral river of idol worship running into my life, be dried up in the name of Jesus. This land shall not be my spiritual burial ground, in Jesus' name. Let all physical and spiritual intruders into my journey be thrown into the Red Sea in the name of Jesus. O Lord God of my glory, I thank you for total victory in the mighty name of Jesus.

Pursue Your Tormentors
With the Fire of God

I declare that I shall not contend with the devil forever. Therefore I decree, O Fire of God, arise with all your weapons of war and pursue my pursuers from this day forth, in the name of Jesus. O Fire of God and east wind of God, arise and pursue my pursuers, in the name of Jesus. O winds of heaven, arise in your hostility and swallow the fire of my enemies, in the name of Jesus. I speak unto the serpent of the Lord in the water to arise, pursue, and swallow up my enemies in the name of Jesus. O morning star, as you are rising today, do not listen to the voice of my enemies, in the name of Jesus. Every power of darkness following my star, receive total insanity in the name of Jesus. Every power of demotion attacking my life, I destroy you; be blotted out of my path by the blood of Jesus and be consumed in the fire of God! I overthrow the table of evil destiny dealers assigned to exchange or trade life and destiny, in Jesus' mighty name! O Lord God to whom all praises belong, receive my gratitude for the answer to my prayers, in the name of Jesus.

Paralyzing evil arrows

I n your light, oh Lord I see light. I now therefore cover myself now with the blood of Jesus. I immerse the totality of my body in the blood of Jesus and I enter the spirit world now to launch a battle against the devil's battle concerning my comfort and well being. All arrows of the enemy fired into my life as a child, be pulled out by fire, in the name of Jesus. Now you arrows of the enemy in my life, go back to your senders and shatter them into desolation, in the name of Jesus. O Lord God of my vengeance, open my eyes to the glory and the portion of your inheritance for me, in the name of Jesus. I break the bow of the enemy, in the name of Jesus. Let my glory grow like a tree planted by the rivers of living waters, in the name of Jesus. Any demonic technology disturbing my upward mobility and social prosperity now, be deprogrammed at once. All satanic aggressions directed toward my peace and harmony, be dissolved by the zeal of the Lord. All you satanic agents summoned to distract me in this battle, I command you to drink the blood of Jesus and be destroyed by it, in the name of Jesus. Any demonic presence or personality assigned to my going out and coming in, receive total blindness in the name of Jesus. All you evil arrows fired into my life, I adjure you by the power in the blood of Jesus, be exposed, be paralyzed, and be destroyed. O weapons of the wicked against me, perish in the name of Jesus. Arrow of the Lord's deliverance, enter the inner chambers of my enemies and scatter them for my sake, in the name of Jesus. I drink of victory in the name of Jesus. Thank you, O man of war, for fighting my battles for me in Jesus' name.

When Facing a Strange Spiritual Attack.

Surely, O Lord, you shall surround me with songs of deliverance. O Lord God of my victories, be my hiding place in the face of every satanic opposition, in the name of Jesus. O Lord God of my strength, give me the power and the anointing without measure to go through the crowd, in Jesus' name. All you enemies of my soul, if I am a servant of God, let fire come down and consume you, after the order of Elijah, the man of God. I am genetically linked to Jesus, therefore I decree that the power of God is upon me. Being filled with the power from on high, I pierce the totality of the armor of the enemy fashioned against me, in the name of Jesus. O Lord God of my salvation, provide me with the Moses to face my Pharaoh and the David to face my Goliath, in the name of Jesus. Let the wheels of all evil chariots pursuing me be caught in a divine mudslide, in the name of Jesus. I pursue and overtake all forces of household wickedness leading away my prosperity and entitlements, and I recover my stolen items from them in Jesus' name. I command all my properties captured by spiritual robbers in my dream to become too hot for them to handle; therefore let all spiritual robbers holding my blessings turn back and return my blessings to me, in the name of Jesus. Let blessings, goodness, and prosperity pursue and overtake me, in the mighty name of Jesus. I send forth the fire of God in the camp of the enemies of my soul at this hour. Let all evil associations against me now be consumed by fire, in the name of Jesus. Angels of the Living God, walk into my life right now with drawn swords and fight for me in the name of Jesus. God is good, the devil is defeated, Jesus is Lord. Thank you, Lord Jesus, for the finished work at the Cross of Calvary.

Let My Stolen Goods and Virtues be Restored

〰️

E very violent wind blowing good things away from my life, be subdued, in the name of Jesus. Let every plan of the enemy to humiliate me be shut down, in the name of Jesus. O Lion of the tribe of Judah, roar in the camp of my enemies and let their hearts melt with fear, in the name of Jesus. Blood of Jesus, swallow all enemy arrows sent in my direction. All evil legs in my events and activities, be cut off in the name of Jesus. O river of God, flow into my life and cleanse me from all spiritual pollution that has entered into my life through the dreams of the night, in the name of Jesus. All favor that has eluded me as a result of pollution in my dreams sent by the forces of darkness, be restored to me in the name of Jesus. I take my dream life back in the midnight battle in the name of Jesus. All darkness surrounding my finances, be removed by the light of God. Lord, increase my brain use, in the name of Jesus. You sword of the Lord, break all soul ties downgrading my life, in the name of Jesus. O Lord God of wonders, connect me with people in high position, influence, and resources for the benefit of your kingdom, in the name of Jesus. Holy Ghost fire, pursue all spiritual thieves that have taken things out of my life. Overtake them and consume them. Let all my stolen goods, properties, and virtues be restored to me in the name of Jesus. Thank you, Lord Jesus, for victories over the power of darkness. Amen.

Arise and Pursue Them!

O Lord God of David, ordain terrifying noises in the camp of my enemies at this hour, in the name of Jesus. Let every kingdom of darkness holding my goods and resources crumble now, in the name of Jesus. I command every satanic hold upon my goodness and prosperity to be scattered into irreparable pieces, in the name of Jesus. Let all entries of attack on my spiritual progress be closed forever, in Jesus' name. Holy Spirit, empower me to pursue my enemies, in the name of Jesus. O Lord God of David, I beseech you by the mercies of heaven, anoint me to pull down all strongholds of the enemies that are standing against me, in the name of Jesus. You thunder fire of God, arise and strike down all demonic strongholds manufactured against me, in the name of Jesus. I command all my imprisoned benefits to be released to me now, in Jesus' name. Praise the Lord with this chorus: *"Great and Mighty is the Lord our God, Great and Mighty is He…"* O Lord God of David, anoint me with the power to pursue, overtake and recover my stolen property from the enemy, in the name of Jesus. O Lord God of my glory, bring to naught every evil counselor and counsel against me, in the name of Jesus. All powers of darkness having a hiding place in my life, vacate once and for all, in the name of Jesus. Let all opportunities of prosperity currently closed to me be opened to me now, in the name of Jesus. You power demon assigned to sit on my prosperity, get off of my finances, in the name of Jesus. Thou spirit of Goliath intimidating my prosperity, receive deadly stones of fire in the name of Jesus. I command all demonic vehicles of transportation carrying away my benefits, to be paralyzed in the name of Jesus. I receive the power to pursue every stubborn pursuer into total confusion, in the name of Jesus. Let the mandate issued to thieves and devourers of my blessings be rendered null and void in Jesus' name. I receive the anointing and power from on high to receive total restoration in all areas of my life, in the name of Jesus. Thank you, Lord Jesus, for setting me free from all forms of bondage.

Going After the Root Cause
of Your Problems

Lord Jesus, give unto me the Spirit of Revelation and Wisdom in the knowledge of you. O arm of the Lord, remove all spiritual cataracts from my eyes, in the name of Jesus. Wisdom of God, open my understanding and teach me deep and secret things of the Lord, in the name of Jesus. Holy Spirit, reveal to me every secret behind all problems that I have, in the name of Jesus. Bring to light, O Lord, everything planned against me in darkness, in the name of Jesus. O Lord, ignite and revive my virtues and potentials in the name of Jesus. Empower me, O Lord, with divine wisdom to do your work, in the name of Jesus. O Light of God, remove all veils of darkness preventing me from having clear spiritual vision, in the name of Jesus. Father, in the name of Jesus, I ask you to reveal your mind to me about *(name a particular decision you need to take)* in Jesus' name. Holy Spirit, reveal deep and secret things to me about *(mention the particular situation)* in the name of Jesus. All you demons that pollute my spiritual visions and dreams, I bind you in the name of Jesus. Let all filthiness blocking my communication with the living God be washed away with the blood of Jesus. I receive power to operate with sharp spiritual eyes that cannot be deceived. Let the glory and the power of the Almighty God fall upon my life in a new way, in the name of Jesus. O Lord Jesus, make me a vessel capable of knowing your secret things. Let a fountain of divine revelations, spiritual visions, dreams and information start to flow in my life continuously, in the name of Jesus. I drink to the full from the well of salvation and anointing of fire in the Holy Ghost, in the name of Jesus. I receive my total freedom from all forms of captivities in the name of Jesus. Thank you, Lord Jesus.

Deliver Me, O Lord, From All Captivity

B lood of Jesus, cleanse me from all filthiness of the spirit, in the name of Jesus. I shall finish every good thing I have laid my hand upon, in the name of Jesus. I shall find favor in my going out and my coming in, the name of Jesus. Let every evil device against my health be disappointed, in Jesus' name. I reject and denounce every spirit of frustration and failure in my life, in the name of Jesus. I overthrow all strongholds of sickness, weakness and fear in my life, in Jesus' name. Holy Spirit, transfuse me now with the blood of the Lord Jesus Christ. Holy Spirit of God, clothe me with the mantle of fire, in the name of Jesus. I reject every spiritual invitation to oppressors in my body, in Jesus' name. O Lord, mighty man of war, make me your battle-axe, in the name of Jesus. Lord Jesus, give me the grace and anointing to live in divine health. Anointing of God, promote me from minimum to maximum in all areas of my life, in Jesus' name. Thank you Lord, for answered prayer, in the name of Jesus.

Speak the Word of His Power

Jehovah El Shaddai, open the pipeline of prosperity into my hand-iwork (mention your handiwork, i.e., ministry, business, professional activity, etc.), in the name of Jesus. Anointing to prosper, fall upon me now, in the name of Jesus. Holy Spirit, take perfect control of my tongue, in the name of Jesus. Lord Jesus, give me the grace to express your love to the needy. I command all contrary trees growing in my life to be uprooted and be consumed by fire, in the name of Jesus. Blessed Heavenly Father, command your blessings of total provision and continuous supply upon me now in Jesus' name. From the north, south, east and west, let all my blessings be released to me in the name of Jesus. I legislate and decree in the heavenlies that all my stolen blessings be restored to me sevenfold at once, in the name of Jesus.

Let all evil attachments to my birthplace be cut off in the name of Jesus. All agents of darkness acting against my breakthroughs, be permanently paralyzed in the name of Jesus. You power of darkness barking against my promotion, be silenced in the name of

Jesus. I receive the anointing for supernatural promotion in all my endeavors, in the name of Jesus. I receive the anointing of the beautiful feet of those who proclaim the gospel of peace, in the name of Jesus. I receive the anointing of the prospering hand, in the name of Jesus. All blockages are now removed. My ship is now coming in with angelic escort, in Jesus' name. Amen.

Let My Promotion Come Forth

First pray for half a session (if your session is an hour, your half a session of 30 minutes) to remove "reproach and contempt," then half a session to release grace, favor and mercy upon your life.

Let all my stolen glory and blessings be restored to me now, in Jesus' name. All invisible evil followers following my destiny, I smite you with the rod of his wrath, in Jesus' name. Let God arise and all the forces of every Pharaoh, Herod and Babylon ruling over my life be scattered in Jesus' name. I release my life from all spiritual cages by the blood of Jesus. Let liquid fire from the Lord pour down on all spiritual thieves stealing good things from my life. With the fetters of God, I bind all powers of darkness delegated to oppress me. I arrest and paralyze every evil architect and evil construction within and around me, in Jesus' name. Let all satanic and human agents issuing word curses against me fall after the order of Balaam, in the name of Jesus. Let all antagonistic social networks of relatives, in-laws, co-workers, unfriendly friends, and their allies warring against me receive divine touch, in Jesus' name. Let every effect of strange handshakes, strange kisses and strange greetings of every kind be nullified in my life and ministry in Jesus' name. Oh goodness of God, fall upon me in the name of Jesus. At any given time, I am flanked by length of days at my right hand, and riches and honor at my left. Long life, be at my right hand, riches and honor be at my left hand. It is well with my soul in Jesus' name. Amen.

Stand in the Gap for Your Children

Heavenly Father, I thank you for blessing me with the children you've blessed me with. Your will for my children is for them to be taught of the Lord. I receive your promise of peace for and upon my children. I declare that the only teaching that will guide my children's life will be the Word of God. I reject all other teachings that the spirit of this age is spreading in our culture, in that they will not register in my children's heart. I therefore I bind every spirit contrary to the Spirit of God preventing me from enjoying my children, in the name of Jesus. I bind every spirit blinding the minds of my children to the Gospel of our Lord Jesus Christ. Let all spirits of stubbornness, pride and disrespect for parents flea from the lives of my children, in the name of Jesus Christ. Father, destroy anything in my children preventing them from doing your will, in the name of Jesus. All curses, evil covenants and inherited problems passed down to my children from past generations be cancelled now in the name of Jesus. Let all evil associations and agreements between my children and my enemies be scattered into desolation, in the name of Jesus. In the name of the Lord Jesus, I declare that my children will not become misdirected arrows. I release my children from the bondage of all evil dominations, in the name of Jesus. Let all evil influences by demonic friends in the lives of my children be neutralized now by the power in the blood of Jesus, in the name of Jesus. You...*(mention the Name of the child),* I dissociate you from any conscious or unconscious demonic groupings or involvement, in the name of Jesus. I receive the mandate to release my children from the prison of any strongman, in the name of Jesus. Let God arise and all the enemies of my home be scattered, in the name of Jesus. All evil influences and activities of strange women (or strange men) on my children, be nullified now in the name of Jesus. I speak to the destiny of my children now and release the covenant of live and peace upon them now, in the name of Jesus.

Instruction: Mention the names of your children one by one and tell the Lord what you want them to become.

You Can Prevail Over Satanic Harassments

R iver of frustration running into my life, dry up in the name of Jesus. I nullify all curses of frustration and failure over my life, in Jesus' name. I pull down all strongholds of failure in my life and ministry, in the name of Jesus. All pipelines of failure into my life, be consumed by fire, in the name of Jesus. All spiritual barriers and limitation to success in my life, be broken into pieces in the name of Jesus. All inherited and self-imposed failure in my life, be consumed by the fire of God, in the name of Jesus. All seeds of failure and frustration in my life, be consumed by the fire of God, in the name of Jesus. Every area of my life that I have lost to failure, be redeemed and restored to me in Jesus' name. You spirit of frustration and failure, loosen your grip over my life in the name of Jesus. I declare this a season of joy and gladness over my life. I decree a continuous season of fulfillment over my life and calling, in the name of Jesus. I proclaim this a season of prosperity and promotion over my life, in the name of Jesus. Amen.

Power Over Sinful Anger

A ny Christian or secular counselor will tell you that almost 90% of all counselees that come to their offices for counseling have problems that originated from the use of sinful anger. What does that mean? It means that anger is the root cause of the majority of problems in people's lives. It also means that *if you don't deal with anger*, anger will deal with you.

Friend, you can't go as far as you want to go in God if you don't prevail over anger. What's more, in your own life, or just looking at the spelling of the world itself, you can see anger is just one letter away from DANGER. Anger can rob you of everything you have in life and in God, and incapacitate your destiny. Pray these prayers aggressively and determine to restructure your life for a positive change. Why pray to overcome anger? Because anger is not something anyone can cast out of you by laying hands on you. YOU and **only you** have the power to deal with it, and with the help of the Holy Spirit you will succeed. It is time to conquer sinful anger. Let's pray!

Instruction: Ask the Lord to forgive you for every fit of anger you have allowed in your life and relationships.

Holy Spirit, help me to crucify my flesh in Jesus' name. Let all the works of the flesh be dismantled in my life, in Jesus' name. Lord Jesus, give me grace to overcome fear, pride and selfishness in my life. Holy Spirit of God, help me to repair all the good things that anger has stolen from my life, in the name of Jesus. O cleansing fire of God, separate me from all works of the flesh, in the name of Jesus. All evil desires and lusts of the flesh in my life, be crucified in the mighty name of Jesus. Lord Jesus, empower me to develop and manifest the fruits of the Spirit. In Jesus' name, I put off anger and quick temperedness and put on tenderheartedness. Lord Jesus, quicken me to hear the voice of the Holy Spirit whenever I am provoked. I exercise my conscience not to take offense, in the name of Jesus. O Lord Jesus, renew a right spirit within me. O Lord Jesus, create in me a new inner man. Song: *Create in Me a Clean Heart, Oh God, and Renew a Right Spirit in Me.* By the power in the name of Jesus, I renounce my right to get angry when confronted with habitual irritants. All roots of irritation that keep anger alive in me, be removed by blood of Jesus. All triggering mechanisms that fuel anger in me, be incapacitated in the name of Jesus. I pull down every thought in my life that says I will never change. All anger that robs me of my miracle, be dismantled in the name of Jesus. Fire of God, remove all veils of darkness from my life, in the name of Jesus. Spirit of self-control, increase in my life, in the name of Jesus. I am free from all sinful anger, in the name of Jesus. I allow only righteous indignation to operate within me, in the name of Jesus. Amen.

Fighting Insomnia
With the Sword of the Spirit

S leeplessness or insomnia is one of the very nasty tactics the enemy of our soul uses to downgrade the quality of our lives. He does this because he knows that if you had a bad night, you're likely to have a bad day. Now is the time to take back your night, so that you can possess your day.

O Ancient of Days, the day is yours and the night belongs to you as well. Therefore take charge of my sleep and watch over me, in the name of Jesus. O Lord God, my defense, surround me with angels of fire with drawn swords each time I sleep, in Jesus' name. Lord Jesus, I cast all my fears, worries and anxieties upon you and take upon myself your peace. All spirits of fear of the dark, insomnia, nervousness, tension, and trepidation tormenting me at night, be dissolved in the blood of Jesus. All tormenting spirits assigned by strange kings to interfere with my dreams of the night, I bind you with chains of fire and fetters of God, in the name of Jesus. Holy Spirit of God, go into all areas of my mind and my subconscious and heal all painful memories and traumas of the past, in the name of Jesus. Lord Jesus, fill me with your love, your peace, and sound sleep as I commit my whole being into your holy hands. I now release myself from the bondage of sleeplessness in the name of Jesus. I break the yoke of the oppressors of the night, in the name of Jesus. I release myself from the bondage of early unprofitable waking up, in the name of Jesus. I sever myself from the bondage of sleeping pills, in the name of Jesus. All sleeplessness attached to previous horrifying experiences in my life, be dismantled now in the name of Jesus. You fear of going to sleep, be eliminated from every area of my life, in the name of Jesus. Lord Jesus, let your name be glorified in every of my life. I receive the peace of God for peaceful sleep, for underneath my pillow are his everlasting arms, in Jesus' name. Amen.

Demolishing Household Wickedness

I withdraw the control of my life from the control and domination of all household wickedness, in the mighty name of Jesus. I withdraw the activities and details of my life from the hands of familiar spirits and household enemies. You strongman delegated over my life, be disgraced, in the name of Jesus. I cut off any problem-inviting link with my parents, in the name of Jesus. Let all bondages of inherited sickness in my life break in the name of Jesus. I withdraw my destiny from the influence and control of household wickedness in the Mighty name of Jesus. Let all evil tongues spreading bad talk about me be completely silenced, in the name of Jesus. I paralyze and frustrate the assignment of envious household enemies against me in the name of Jesus. All powers and vessels sitting on my well being and prosperity, be violently overthrown in the name of Jesus. Let all evil expectations of the enemy against my life perish, in the name of Jesus. All money-consuming demons attached to my finances, I cut you off, in the name of Jesus. All satanic strategies delaying my miracle, be frustrated in the name of Jesus.

All my miracles that are held by household wickedness, be released to me now in the name of Jesus. I declare that I am spiritually linked to Jesus. I belong to Jesus, therefore I reject evil effects of household wickedness upon my life. I reap the reward of my inheritance of life and peace in Christ Jesus. Amen.

It is Your Time to Receive Favor

F avor of God, fall upon me in the name of Jesus. Let all demonic obstacles that have been established in the heart of (insert name) against my prosperity, be destroyed in the name of Jesus. Lord Jesus, show (insert name) dreams, visions and restlessness that would advance my cause, in the name of Jesus. I break asunder all networks of slandering spirits against me, in the name of Jesus. Holy Spirit, bring my name favorably into the mind of potential helpers, in the name of Jesus. Fire of the Holy Spirit, purge my life from all evil marks put upon me, in the name of Jesus.

O hyssop of God, cleanse me from all reproach and contempt in the name of Jesus. Spring up, O fountain of favor, and flow into my life in the name of Jesus.

Smashing Addiction on the Head

The following session will help you combat all life-dominating sins and harmful habits: alcoholism, smoking, gambling, substance abuse, including food addictions, television, emotional shopping, phone talk addictions, etc. Behind every addiction, there is an evil authority giving you evil commands to do things you know deep down within yourself you shouldn't be doing, or that you don't want to do. By taking authority over that evil authority, you will overcome these harmful habits.

The *first exercise* we are going to do in this session is to pray the doctrinal prayer in the next paragraph. When we say "doctrinal prayer," we mean that the statements you are about to make are legally settled matters in the spirit world and binding in the spirit realm, and the devil cannot dispute or resist them. Do you remember when the Lord Jesus used the famous three "It is written" to defeat Satan's strategies? Yes, those were doctrinal statements to fight Satan. You are going to use the same tools in the following session to fight the strongman delegated to cripple your well being and prosperity. A doctrinal prayer is also a prayer of authority (as in the following paragraph).

Let's pray:

Satan, in the name of the Lord Jesus Christ, the resurrected Son of the Living God, I put you and all your legions on notice that I am attacking you from my position of power and authority, in Christ Jesus, at the right hand of the Father, in the third heaven. This places me high above you, your principalities, powers, thrones, dominions, world rulers, rulers of darkness, kings, princes and every angelic rank under command.

Heavenly Father, dispatch mighty angels for my sake now to dismantle all forces of darkness in the second heaven that want to oppose these prayers. Thank You, Lord, for divine protection. Thank you, Lord, for sending me reinforcement of angels as needed. In Jesus' name, I pray.

In standing position, raise your left hand toward heaven (it is a sign to the enemy that you are placing judgment upon him) and declare:

"You evil authority giving me evil commands, be subdued, in the name of Jesus!" Repeat this several times, authoritatively, for 30 minutes or more.

Call the spirit you do not desire in your life by name. Then issue the following command firmly and repeatedly, "You evil spirit of (name evil spirit), I command you to come out of my life, in the name of the Lord Jesus!"

Pray as in the following example: "You spirit of nicotine (or it could be junk food, watching horror movies hours without end, or negative talk, etc.), come out of my brain, mind and body in the name of Jesus. I loose myself from you. With the sword of the Lord, I cut off your grip over my emotions. I destroy your habitation in the seat of my emotions. I command you to leave me right now, in the mighty name of our Lord Jesus Christ.

"With the sword of God in my hand, I come against all networks of associated spirits dwelling my stomach, my intestine, my bloodstream, my lungs, my sinuses, my throat and any system of my body to prolong addiction in my life. I come against gluttony, moodiness and mood swings, restlessness, uncontrollable cravings, nervousness, fear, sweet tooth, self-reward, self-pity, lying and the likes (add more spirits if you need to), in the authority of the name of Jesus.

"Holy Spirit, send forth angels of God to wash my mind, my heart, my emotions, with the blood of Jesus. Lord Jesus, restore the seat of emotions to its original spot in my life. Holy Spirit, restore my mind, and let this mind in Christ be now in me. Lord Jesus, take total authority and control of my mind from this day forth. I claim victory over mind-controlling spirits operating against me, in the name of Jesus. I am more than a conqueror, in Jesus' name."

Pray in tongues for 15 minutes or more. Sing one or two songs of praise and thanksgiving. Thank the Lord in faith for answering your prayers

Dealing with Depression and the Spirit of Heaviness

I t is written, "On Mount Zion, there shall be deliverance." Therefore, I have come to Mount Zion for my deliverance. Hear me, all you spirits of oppression and heaviness tormenting me, I resist you. The Word of God is against you. The Bible says, "Submit to God, resist the devil, and he must flee…" I submit to God and I resist you, spirit of heaviness and deep sleep. Therefore, you must flee away from me now, in the name of Jesus. O arm of the Lord, remove all roots of spiritual heaviness and depression from my life, in the name of Jesus. O Captain of the Lord's army, close now and forever all gates I have opened to any spirit of oppression in my life, in the name of Jesus. Lord Jesus, walk back into my past and heal all wounded memories and bruised emotions, in the name of Jesus. Arise, O Lord, man of war, and scatter all powers of darkness tormenting my spiritual well being, in the name of Jesus.

I resist and bind every spirit of fear, discouragement, self-pity and depression, in the name of Jesus. I claim the spirit of power, of love, of a calm and well-balanced mind in the name of Jesus. All rivers of sorrow and sadness flowing into my life, dry up in the name of Jesus. I reject all evil commands from evil authorities, and I nullify such orders and command now, in the name of Jesus. You, my inner man, I command you to arise from the shell of heaviness and depression, in the name of Jesus. Blood of Jesus, redeem my mind, in the name of Jesus. Thank you, Lord God of deliverance, for setting me free from every evil work, in the name of Jesus.

Confronting Mind Control

I f there is any spirit that is tormenting people today more than any other, it is this spirit of mind control. In Satan's administration, mind control works under witchcraft. Mind control is an errand boy to witchcraft. When mind control is sent against someone, it takes over people's faculty and ability to think clearly on their own. A person under the influence of mind control often makes irrational decisions, and turns to very, very irrational options when faced with a crisis or even in their normal daily activities. People under captivity of a mind control spirit are also often confused, unable to make decision for themselves, constantly crying. It is time to take authority through prayer over this witchcraft attack.

I cover my mind with the blood of Jesus. I resist and refuse all bewitchment of my mind. I withdraw my mind from the control of all witchcraft spirits and I pull down the stronghold of confusion in my life, in the name of Jesus. All strongholds of confusion in my life, be demolished in the name of Jesus. Let the storm of confusion within my mind be silenced, in the name of Jesus. All clouds of confusion that have enveloped my mind, fade away now, in the name of Jesus. I reject all storms of confusion assigned against me, in the name of Jesus. I claim a sound mind in the name of Jesus. All powers of darkness that want to destroy my life, go back to your sender, in the name of Jesus. All arrows of mind manipulation fired into my life, go back to our sender in the name of Jesus. You, my mind, reject evil arrows, in the name of Jesus. I receive a divine touch of healing and restoration in the name of Jesus. Lord Jesus, strengthen me in my mind with your fire and your power. All strong-holds of uncontrollable thoughts in my life, be pulled down, in the name of Jesus. All evil imaginations in my heart, be cast down in the name of Jesus. All areas of my thought life, I bring you into the obe-dience of Christ and his Word, in the name of Jesus. All evil remote control powers over my thought life, I cut you off, in the name of Jesus. I seal off all doorways of evil, uncontrollable thoughts in my life with the blood of Jesus. I cast down all imaginations contrary to my prayer life, in the name of Jesus. I crush all demonic imagina-tions and evil expectations, and I put on the mind of Christ Jesus. I immunize my spirit, soul and body with the mind of Christ against every vain imagination, in the name of Jesus. All evil imaginations against me, be scattered in the name of Jesus. I frustrate all satanic imaginations against my life, in the name of Jesus. I pull down all strongholds of the enemy in my life, in the name of Jesus. I pull down all demonic ladders the enemy is using to climb into my life, in the name of Jesus. All demonic ladders into my life, be roasted by fire and be destroyed in the name of Jesus. All satanic assignments and orders commissioned against me, be arrested and be cancelled, in the name of Jesus. I take captive all evil thoughts in my heart and mind and cast them down now, in the Jesus' name. Blood of Jesus, cleanse my heart from all evil thoughts. My heart, be delivered from all evil thoughts, in the name of Jesus. I shield my heart with the fire of God from all evil thoughts, in the name of Jesus. You habitation of darkness in my heart, be desolate, in the name of Jesus. All evil attacks on my mind, be frustrated, in the name of Jesus. All satanic tables upon which the devil exhibits its evil in my heart, be overthrown by the thunder of God, in the name of Jesus. Arrows of fear, frustration, worry, anxiety, burden fired into my mind, be pulled out by fire, in the name of Jesus. Holy Ghost fire, stir up my pure mind in the name of Jesus. You powers of witchcraft bent to corrupt my desire and my pure mind, be roasted by fire, in the name of Jesus. You strongman of evil imagination paralyzing my thought life, depart from my life, in the name of Jesus. All evil trees in my mind, be removed by the fire of God, in the name of Jesus. I uproot all hidden evil trees in my mind, in the name of Jesus. You evil fruit in my life, die in the name of Jesus. You planter of evil trees in my life, be roasted by fire, in the name of Jesus. I bind and cast down the spirit of uncertainty in my mind, in Jesus' name. Holy Ghost fire, come and occupy all areas of my mind vacated by the spirit of uncertainty. You mind-controlling and mind-blanking spirit, you will not prosper in my life, in the name of Jesus. My mind, I command you to think right thoughts, in the name of Jesus. Lord Jesus, soak my mind with heavenly revelations. I gather together all areas of my mind that have been scattered, in the name of Jesus. Arrows of the enemy fired into my mind, I fire you back into the camp of your senders, in the name of Jesus. I command you, my mind, go back to your original state at creation. You, my mind, I command you to be renewed and restored in the name of Jesus. By faith, I release my mind from the grip of the spirits of: pride, vanity, greed, fear, violence, worry, envy, laziness, depression, confusion, self-importance, bitterness, carnal imaginations, deception, wicked imaginations, ignorance, condemnation, arrogance, forgetfulness, mind-blanking, mind dullness, turmoil, incoherence, ambivalence, indecision, compromise, giving up, uncertainty, self-pity, unworthiness, self-criticism, and low-self-esteem, in Jesus' name. Father, in the name of Jesus, I invite the ministry of great deliverance into my mind now. You powers of darkness, loose your control over my mind, in the name of Jesus. Let my carnal mind, which is at war with God, be conquered and be at peace with God, in the name of Jesus. I cast down all vain imaginations working against my mind, in the name of Jesus. I recover and possess all good things lost to the spirit of uncertainty, in the name of Jesus. All great ideas that have evaporated from my life, return to me and be restored back into my life, in the name of Jesus. All the good thoughts that the strongman has paralyzed in my life, receive life and be restored back into my life, in the name of Jesus.

TESTIMONIALS

Dear fellow laborer in His vineyard:
If these prayers are a blessing to you, we want to hear from you.

1) Send us a testimony report of what the Lord has done for you through these prayers.

2) If you want us to bring our deliverance workshop into your city, let us know by email or by phone.

3) If you want us to bring these prayers to your church, to ignite or re-ignite the fire of the Holy Spirit therein, let us know as well by email or by phone.

4) If you feel led by the Holy Spirit to order this spiritual warfare prayer book, and to bless someone with it, let us know, and we will be glad to send it to them on your behalf.

5) If you have any questions, concerns or comments as it concerns these prayers, please contact us. We want to hear from you.

Your Name:

Your Mailing address:

Your email address:

Tel 1:

Tel 2:

You may send your testimonies, comments, praise reports, or questions, to:

Rev. Joseph A. DODJRO

Exhorter, Prophetic Intercessor, Deliverance minister

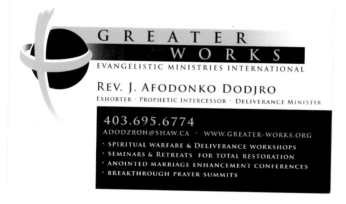

GREATER WORKS
EVANGELISTIC MINISTRIES INTERNATIONAL
REV. J. AFODONKO DODJRO
EXHORTER · PROPHETIC INTERCESSOR · DELIVERANCE MINISTER
403.695.6774
ADODZROH@SHAW.CA · WWW.GREATER-WORKS.ORG
· SPIRITUAL WARFARE & DELIVERANCE WORKSHOPS
· SEMINARS & RETREATS FOR TOTAL RESTORATION
· ANOINTED MARRIAGE ENHANCEMENT CONFERENCES
· BREAKTHROUGH PRAYER SUMMITS